全国高职高专"十二五"规划教材

New Practical College English
新编实用大学英语（第二册）
学生用书

主　编　黄　芳　张　高

副主编　何文婷　娄佳丽　杜　恒

编　者　陈　娟　方　珍　杨玉洁

　　　　张丽萍　胡　燕　李　蓉

中国水利水电出版社
www.waterpub.com.cn

内 容 提 要

《新编实用大学英语》是由长期从事一线教学的大学英语教师，结合多年的教学经验，以教育部颁发的《高职高专教育英语课程教育基本要求》为依据，充分考虑高职学生的基础和特点的一套内容更实用、形式更创新的高职高专教材。

全书共 8 个单元，供第二学期使用。每个单元按照听说（Listening & Speaking），课文（Passages），语法（Grammar），写作（Writing）和轻松一刻（Enjoy Yourselves）五个板块的顺序安排。每个板块围绕主题，结合高职高专学生的特点及今后工作需要，设有相关专项训练，并在教材末附有大学英语二、三级考试模拟题各一套，以供学生自我检测。

本书馈赠超值 MP3 光盘，录音主要由专业人士录制。

图书在版编目（CIP）数据

新编实用大学英语. 第2册 / 黄芳, 张高主编. --
北京：中国水利水电出版社, 2015.1 (2018.1 重印)
全国高职高专"十二五"规划教材. 学生用书
ISBN 978-7-5170-2775-1

Ⅰ. ①新… Ⅱ. ①黄… ②张… Ⅲ. ①英语－高等职业教育－教材 Ⅳ. ①H31

中国版本图书馆CIP数据核字(2014)第308666号

策划编辑：寇文杰　　责任编辑：邓建梅　　加工编辑：于丽娜　　封面设计：李　佳

书　　名	全国高职高专"十二五"规划教材 新编实用大学英语（第二册）学生用书
作　　者	主　编　黄　芳　张　高 副主编　何文婷　娄佳丽　杜　恒
出版发行	中国水利水电出版社 （北京市海淀区玉渊潭南路1号D座　100038） 网址：www.waterpub.com.cn E-mail：mchannel@263.net（万水） 　　　　sales@waterpub.com.cn 电话：（010）68367658（发行部）、82562819（万水）
经　　售	北京科水图书销售中心（零售） 电话：（010）88383994、63202643、68545874 全国各地新华书店和相关出版物销售网点
排　　版	北京万水电子信息有限公司
印　　刷	三河市铭浩彩色印装有限公司
规　　格	184mm×240mm　16开本　11.25印张　246千字
版　　次	2015年1月第1版　2018年1月第3次印刷
印　　数	7501—10000 册
定　　价	26.00元（赠MP3光盘）

凡购买我社图书，如有缺页、倒页、脱页的，本社发行部负责调换

版权所有·侵权必究

前　　　言

随着高考制度的革新以及大学英语教学改革的不断深入，高职院校对其教材的改革也在不断地探索和创新。为此，我们编写了《新编实用大学英语》，期望在满足高职学生对大学英语多元化的需求基础之上，提高学生的英语应用能力。具体而言，本教材具有如下特点：

（1）紧扣大纲，结合四川省大学英语等级考试要求编写。《基本要求》和《考试大纲》是我们选材的主要依据，同时整套教材各单元听、说、读、写、译都围绕同一主题展开。

（2）选材新颖，结合学生心理需求。结合高职高专学生的兴趣，本教材所有课文都选自最新的报刊杂志、网络文章及经典美文，趣味性强；练习形式也较之以往的教材有所突破，除了传统训练形式外，本教材还将"托业"考试及全国大学英语竞赛中的 IQ 测试引入各单元，同时各单元末以"轻松一刻"结束本单元的学习，使学生能体会学习的乐趣。

（3）实效性强，考学练融为一体。教材的所有编者皆为经验丰富的一线教师，对高职高专学院教学现状和学生的需求有一定的了解，能针对问题，有的放矢地提供解决方案。在练习的形式上与英语等级考试接轨，以有效解决应试培训与常规教学所引发的课时矛盾。

（4）重视应用能力培养，为后续教育奠定基础。应用能力是指运用语言的能力，既包含语言的基本应用能力，又包括实际的涉外能力，即跨文化交际能力。为达到这一目标，在听说训练方面的选材即要求生活化，又力求体现"文化"差异；在读写译方面也尽量以实用性为重心进行编写。"学以致用，为后续课程奠定基础"是我们编写教材的宗旨。

《新编实用大学英语》由一、二两册及配套练习册组成。本书为《新编实用大学英语》第二册，共 8 个单元，供第二学期使用。

本册每个单元包括听说（Listening & Speaking），课文（Passages），语法（Grammar），写作（Writing）和轻松一刻（Enjoy Yourselves）五个板块。

Listening & Speaking 分为 2 个部分——听力和会话。听力部分共设 3 个练习。通过对话、短文理解和听写填空三种形式训练并提高学生的听力能力。会话部分共设 2 个练习，主要是给学生创造一个活用所学内容的机会。

Passages 部分内容广泛，共配有 2 篇课文和相关练习。

Passage One 为精读材料。教师在教学过程中，应该充分利用每单元的 Warm-up Question。该练习能够起到引入课文，活跃气氛，启发思想的作用。本书 Passage One 和 Passage Two 后的生词表将单词、词组和专有名词分别列出。配合 Passage One 的练习共包括 Read and Think，Read and Try，Read and Translate，Reading Skills 等项。

Passage Two 为泛读材料，是与单元内容相关的补充阅读。目的在于扩大学生的知识面，提高学生的阅读能力。

Grammar 以系统复习英语语法为主，练习重点放在学生容易混淆，容易出错的语法现象上。

Writing 是根据学生应试及实践需要而编写的实用写作训练，旨在培养学生模拟套写常用应用文的能力。

Enjoy Yourselves 每单元选配一篇短小精悍的幽默故事、文化背景知识或者一首好听的英文歌曲等，培养学生学习、体味与欣赏英语和英美文化的能力。

《新编实用大学英语》由四川职业技术学院黄芳、张高担任主编，负责全书的设计、编排和书稿的审定。教材第二册由黄芳、张高主编，黄芳（第一单元）、陈娟（第二单元）、方珍（第三单元）、杨玉洁（第四、六单元）、张高（第五单元）、张丽萍（第七单元）、胡燕（第八单元）、李蓉（模拟题）等老师参加了改编，罗峰、苏雪莲、付志扬、吴疆、杜恒、雷惠麟、何文婷、孟青兰、卢虹、郑瑜、曾慧彬、娄佳丽、雷雯、宋佳玲等老师也参加了资料的收集、筛选、校对等修编工作。

此教材的编写思路来源于教学实践，也需要在教学实践中得到检验。实际编写过程中如有疏漏和不当之处，望广大师生批评指正！

编 者

2014 年 12 月

目 录

前言

Unit One　Social Issues

Section I　Listening & Speaking ·················· 1
Section II　Passage One ··························· 5
　　Let's Marry to Keep the Love Going ······· 5
Section II　Passage Two ·························· 10
　　Becoming a Mortgage Slave or Not ········ 10
Section III　Grammar ····························· 14
　　Infinitive（不定式）···························· 14
Section IV　Writing ······························· 15
　　Invitation Card/ Letter（请柬）··············· 15
Section V　Enjoy Yourselves ···················· 17

Unit Two　Life Experience

Section I　Listening & Speaking ················ 18
Section II　Passage One ·························· 21
　　The Art of Living ······························ 21
Section II　Passage Two ·························· 26
　　7 Ways to Find Out What You Really Want in Life · 26
Section III　Grammar ····························· 30
　　Participle（分词）······························ 30
Section IV　Writing ······························· 31
　　Business Card（名片）·························· 31
Section V　Enjoy Yourselves ···················· 32
　　Funny Pictures ································ 32

Unit Three　Environment

Section I　Listening & Speaking ················ 33
Section II　Passage One ·························· 37
　　Healthy Lifestyle Helping to Protect the
　　Environment ·································· 37
　　Context Clues to Word Meaning ············ 41
Section II　Passage Two ·························· 42
　　Protection of the Environment ············· 42
Section III　Grammar ····························· 46
　　Gerund（动名词）······························ 46
Section IV　Writing ······························· 47
　　Note for Leaving（请假条）··················· 47
Section V　Enjoy Yourselves ···················· 48
　　A Joke ··· 48

Unit Four　Transportation

Section I　Listening & Speaking ················ 49
Section II　Passage One ·························· 52
　　The Impact of High-Speed Rail on Civil Aviation ··· 52
Section II　Passage Two ·························· 58
　　Children Say They Prefer Daddy to Drive ········ 58
Section III　Grammar ····························· 62
　　Noun Clauses（名词性从句）·················· 62
Section IV　Writing ······························· 63
　　Poster（海报）································· 63
Section V　Enjoy Yourselves ···················· 64
　　The Origin of Hot Dogs ······················ 64

Unit Five　Science & Technology

Section I　Listening & Speaking ················ 66
Section II　Passage One ·························· 70
　　Wash. U. Scientists Discover Mind-Reading ······· 70

Section II　Passage Two ·············· 75
　　Exploring 3D Technology: From Cinema to Home · 75
Section III　Grammar ················· 79
　　Attributive Clause（定语从句）··········· 79
Section IV　Writing ··················· 81
　　Certificates（证明）··················· 81
Section V　Enjoy Yourselves ·········· 82
　　Chinese Term ······················· 82

Unit Six　History

Section I　Listening & Speaking ······ 83
Section II　Passage One ·············· 87
　　150th Anniversary of the U.S. Civil War ········· 87
Section II　Passage Two ·············· 93
　　American History Lessons ············· 93
Section III　Grammar ················· 97
　　Adverbial Clause（状语从句）··········· 97
Section IV　Writing ··················· 98
　　Advertisement（广告）················· 98
Section V　Enjoy Yourselves ·········· 99
　　Lines in the Film of "The Spy Next Door" ········· 99

Unit Seven　Literature

Section I　Listening & Speaking ······ 102
Section II　Passage One ·············· 106
　　Three Days to See ··················· 106
Section II　Passage Two ·············· 111
　　About Reading Books ················ 111

Section III　Grammar ················· 116
　　Inversion（倒装）···················· 116
Section IV　Writing ··················· 117
　　Business Letter（商务信函）··········· 117
Section V　Enjoy Yourselves ·········· 119
　　A poem ···························· 119

Unit Eight　News

Section I　Listening & Speaking ······ 120
Section II　Passage One ·············· 123
　　Meet Disney Characters in Shanghai ······ 123
Section II　Passage Two ·············· 129
　　Migrants to be Quizzed on English Skills
　　before Benefits ····················· 129
Section III　Grammar ················· 133
　　Agreement（一致）··················· 133
Section IV　Writing ··················· 134
　　News（新闻）······················· 134
Section V　Enjoy Yourselves ·········· 135
　　Everytime ·························· 135

Appendix 1　Simulated Tests

Test One (Band Two) ················· 137
Test Two (Band Three) ··············· 149

Appendix 2

Words and Expressions ··············· 161
Phrases and Expressions ············· 172

Unit One Social Issues

➢ Warm-up Question

Are there any social issues in China? What do you think of them?

# Section I Listening & Speaking

◆ Listening

Task 1.

Directions: In this section, you will hear 6 short conversations. At the end of each conversation, a question will be asked about what was said. Both the conversation and the question will be spoken twice. After each question there will be a pause. During the pause you must read the four choices marked A), B), C) and D), and decide which is the best answer. Then mark your answer.

Example:
You will hear:
M: Is it possible for you to work late, Miss Green?
W: Work late? I suppose so, if you really think it's necessary.
Q: Where does the conversation most probably take place?

You will read:
A) At the office.
B) In the waiting room.
C) At the airport.
D) In a restaurant.

From the conversation, we know that the two were talking about some work they had to finish in the evening. This is most likely to have taken place at the office. Therefore, A) "At the office" is the best answer. You should choose answer A).

Sample Answer:

A)   B)   C)   D)

New Words and Expressions

reservation [ˌrezəˈveɪʃn]   *n.* 预订

cigarette [ˌsɪɡəˈret]   *n.* 香烟；纸烟

counter [ˈkaʊntə(r)]   *n.* （商店、银行等的）柜台

telegram [ˈtelɪɡræm]   *n.* 电报（用电信号传递的信息）

a front view 临街面

a rear view 背街面

make-up 化妆品

Now let us listen to 6 short conversations, both the conversation and the question will be spoken twice.

1. A) A restaurant.　　　　　　　　　　B) A park.
   C) A hotel.　　　　　　　　　　　　D) A school.
2. A) To make a reservation.　　　　　　B) To have a drink.
   C) To look through the list.　　　　　D) To fill out a form.
3. A) The one with a window.　　　　　 B) The one with a beautiful view.
   C) The one with a front view.　　　　D) The one with a rear view.
4. A) The room number is 4047.　　　　 B) The room is on the 4th floor.
   C) The daily rate is ＄115.　　　　　D) The room number is 1447.
5. A) Foreign cigarettes.　　　　　　　 B) Chinese cigarettes.
   C) Some make-up.　　　　　　　　　D) Some cigarettes and make-up.
6. A) Two letters and one telegram.　　　B) A message.
   C) Two letters, one telegram and a message. D) Two letters and two telegrams.

Task 2.

Directions: In this section, you will hear a short passage. At the end of the passage, you will hear two questions. Both the passage and the questions will be spoken twice. After you hear one question, you must choose the best answer from the four choices marked A), B), C) and D). Then mark your answer.

New Words and Expressions

consumer [kən'sjuːmə(r)]   *n.* 消费者；顾客
persuade [pə'sweɪd]   *v.* 劝说；说服
create [krɪ'eɪt]   *v.* 创造；创作；创建
environment [ɪn'vaɪrənmənt]   *n.* 环境；客观环境
exception [ɪk'sepʃn]   *n.* 不包括在内的人（或物）；例外

1. A) Advertisements also provide money for newspapers, magazines, radios and TV stations, etc.
   B) Advertisements give the latest information about products.
   C) In a shop as more goods are old, they have to be sold cheaply.
   D) Consumers could not know about goods in their local shops, if there were no advertising.

2. A) Advertisements suggest people not to buy goods.
   B) Advertisements make the price of all the products higher and higher.
   C) Advertisements are not only necessary but also helpful.
   D) Advertisements beautify the environment.

Task 3.

A. Directions: In this section, you will hear a passage three times. Listen carefully during the first reading. Then listen to the passage again. When it is being read the second time, you should fill in the ten blanks numbered from S1) to S10) with the exact words or phrases you have just heard. Finally, when the passage is read for the third time, you should check what you have written.

New Words and Expressions

advertisement [əd'vɜːtɪsmənt]   *n.* 广告；启事
make money 挣钱

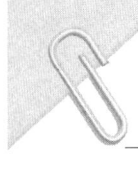

Nowadays advertisements are everywhere. I think advertisements have both good and bad **S1)** _____ on young students.

On one hand, advertisements give us information about things to buy. They make it easier for us to choose the best product. Also, some advertisements are beautifully **S2)** _____ and pleasant to look at.

But on the other hand, they can make trouble for us. First, most advertisements look **S3)** _____ and they persuade us to buy things we don't need at all. This is **S4)** _____ bad for young people. They have not made money yet and they have to ask for money from their parents. Sometimes they buy lots of **S5)** _____ food because the advertisements look **S6)** _____. We know junk food is always not **S7)** _____. What's more, some advertisements don't tell the truth. Many people find themselves **S8)** _____ after using certain products.

In short, advertisements have pros and **S9)** _____. As young students, we should learn to **S10)** _____ the problems ourselves.

B. Listen to the passage again and then decide whether each of the following statements is true (T) or false (F).

1. (   ) The writer thinks advertisements only have bad effects on young students.
2. (   ) The advertisements can make trouble for us.
3. (   ) Sometimes the students buy lots of junk food.
4. (   ) Some advertisements don't tell the truth to the public.

◆ **Speaking**

Task 1. Talk about the social issues with your classmates.

Task 2. Two students are in a pair to make a conversation as the following sample.

Sample

A: Congratulations! I heard that you're going to have the wedding ceremony. When is it?

B: We haven't fixed yet. You see it is one of the most important events in our life, and there are a lot of things to sort out.

A: Are you going to have a big wedding?

B: Yes, we are. Could you be my bridesmaid?

A: Sure, my pleasure.

Unit One　Social Issues

Section II　Passage One

Let's Marry to Keep the Love Going

The hectic lifestyle today posts that many people just do not have the time for marathon love to find their ideal partner. In my opinion, there is not much difference between being in love and marriage. As the old saying goes: marriage is just the days after a love certificate.

I think most people tend to get married after they fall in love, i. e. they love each other and intend to keep the love forever. If you really meet someone you fall in love with immediately, why not marry him/her soon? There is no difference in the two issues for real love.

People who choose a "Flash Marriage" believe there is no time for marathon dating when there are so many other things to be done. In addition, the issue of love is not an affair that can be guaranteed forever. Even after dating for five or eight years, nobody is confident that the love will be everlasting. If they spend a long time testing the affection, it's just to put obstacles on their own way. If the affection can't go on forever, both sides will be deeply hurt and no one can relive their past youth. Therefore, if you fall in love with someone, marry him/her, other things can be thought about later. No matter whether it is for dating or marriage, love is the most important thing.

If they are unfortunate to put an end to the wedlock, "Flash Marriage" and "Flash Divorce" are also "trouble-free". Since if the "Flash Marriage" couple divorces, they will feel less hurt when compared with those who have been together for a long time.

So, "Flash Marriage" seems more like a big gamble. Perhaps "Flash Marriage" is not suitable for everyone. Only those who have courage and right attitude can take the risk!

(Words 302)

（节选自《英语畅谈流行时尚 50 主题》，主编　谭晓东）

New Words（★三级词汇　◆超纲词汇）

◆hectic ['hektɪk]　*a.* 忙碌的，繁忙的
　marathon ['mærəθən]　*n.* 马拉松赛跑（距离约 42 公里，合 26 英里）
　partner ['pɑ:tnə(r)]　*n.* 配偶；同伴

marriage ['mærɪdʒ]　*n.* 结婚；婚姻
★certificate [sə'tɪfɪkət]　*n.* 证明；证明书
★tend [tend]　*v.* 往往会；常常就；趋向
intend [ɪn'tend]　*v.* 打算；计划；想要
flash [flæʃ]　*n.* 闪光；闪耀
　　　　　　　v. （使）闪耀，闪光；用光发出信号
guarantee [ˌɡærən'tiː]　*n.* 保证；担保
　　　　　　　　　　　v. 保证；担保
confident ['kɒnfɪdənt]　*a.* 自信的；有自信心的
everlasting [ˌevə'lɑːstɪŋ]　*a.* 永久的；永恒的
◆affection [ə'fekʃn]　*n.* 喜爱；钟爱
◆obstacle ['ɒbstəkl]　*n.* 障碍；阻碍
◆relive [ˌriː'lɪv]　*v.* （尤指在想象中）再次体验，重温；回味
◆wedlock ['wedlɒk]　*n.* 婚姻；已婚状态
divorce [dɪ'vɔːs]　*n.* 离婚
　　　　　　　　v. 与（某人）离婚；判（某人）离婚
gamble ['ɡæmbl]　*v.* （牌戏、赛马等中）赌博，打赌
　　　　　　　　n. 赌博；打赌；冒险
suitable ['suːtəbl]　*a.* 合适的；适宜的
risk [rɪsk]　*n.* 危险；风险
　　　　　　v. 使……冒风险（或面临危险）

Phrases and Expressions

have the time for...to do sth. 有时间做某事
in one's opinion 在某人看来
get married 结婚
fall in love 相爱
intend to do sth. 打算做某事
marathon dating 马拉松式约会
guarantee sth. (to sb.) 向某人保证某事
be guaranteed to do sth. 必定做某事
spend...(in) doing sth. 花……（时间、金钱等）做某事
no matter whether 无论是否……（都不要紧）
compare with 与……相比较

Unit One   Social Issues

Read and Think

I. Answer the following questions according to the passage.
1. Why do some people think that there is not much difference between being in love and marriage?
2. Why some people choose "flash marriage"?
3. Is it easy for "flash marriage" couple to end their marriage if they have to divorce?

Read and Try

II. Fill in each blank with a right word in its right form using the words in the following box.

| marriage | certificate | issue | attitude |
| compare | confident | suitable | affection |

1. Mother often _____ me with my sister.
2. As a landlady, Alice always takes a maternal _____ toward the Chinese girl.
3. Tom is praying in the temple for his son to get a wonderful _____.
4. The old man has a great _____ for his hometown.
5. He was just not _____ for the job because of his carelessness.
6. To obtain a passport, you have to send in your birth _____ with the form.
7. They are _____ of success.
8. They have published a lot of new books on international _____.

III. There are eight incomplete sentences below. For each sentence, there are four choices marked A), B), C) and D). You should choose the proper one to complete each sentence.
1. He is looking for a wife but he hasn't found his _____ mate.
   A) idea   B) idealism
   C) ideal   D) ideas
2. Lily wants to _____ her husband.
   A) leave   B) divorce
   C) divorced   D) depart from
3. The TV set has a year's _____.
   A) guarantor   B) guard
   C) guardian   D) guarantee
4. _____ this style with that one, and you will see which is better.

A) Comparing	B) Compare
C) Compared	D) To compare

5. I_____ study abroad.

A) intend	B) intend to
C) intending	D) to be intended

6. _____ French, he has to study Japanese and German.

A) In addition to	B) Beside
C) Beside of	D) In addition

7. Though it was Sunday yesterday, I had a _____ day in the office.

A) hector	B) hectoring
C) hectare	D) hectic

8. A thought _____ through my mind.

A) dodge	B) flashed
C) sparkled	D) lighting

Read and Translate

IV. Translate the following sentences into English.

1. 恐怕我的英语同她的英语相比要差得多。(compare with)
2. 今天除了做家庭作业，他还得学英语。(in addition to)
3. 肯定是要下雨的。(be guaranteed to)
4. 在英国小雨和本相遇后很快坠入了爱河。(fall in love)

Reading Skills

Specific Information

Sometimes you only need to find detail information concerning when, where, what, who, or how in a piece of writing. In search of these data, you must be careful about the exactness of the specific information.

Directions: Read the following paragraphs carefully, and then choose the best answer.
Passage One

I must say that my greatest interest in life is studying. I would rather study than anything else. Since I left school, I have taken courses in all sorts of things. Once or twice I have done a correspondence course, but I much prefer evening classes because it's more fun that way. My latest "craze"－if you can call it that－is foreign languages. I'm learning two, not one!

(Words 71)

Unit One Social Issues

1. Since the author left school, he has _____.
   A) taken a lot of correspondence courses
   B) attended many different courses
   C) learned a lot of languages
   D) had many interests

   Passage Two

   The job interview is the time to "sell" yourself by giving examples of experiences you have had about the job and by showing your good points. It is a good idea to make a list of your job experiences or a list of school courses that prepared you for the job. Be honest, but show confidence in yourself and your ability to do the job.

   (Words 65)

2. When you are preparing for a job interview, you'd better _____.
   A) show confidence
   B) give examples of your job-related experiences
   C) believe yourself
   D) make a list of your job experiences or a list of school courses

   Passage Three

   Adult drivers listen to music on the car radio as they drive to work. They also listen to the news about sports, the weather, and the life of American people. Most of the radio programmes are music. Pop or popular music singers make much money. They make a CD or a tape which radio stations use in many places. Once the popular singer is heard all over the country, young people buy his or her tape. Some of the money from these tapes comes to the singer. Wherever the singer goes, all the young people want to meet him or her. Now the singer has become a national star.

   (Words 108)

3. When pop singers _____, they will become national stars.
   A) make much money
   B) make a CD or tape
   C) are loved by all the young people
   D) are wanted to sing on the radio

   Passage Four

   It was reported that the number of deaths caused by railways in one year was 4,712. That sounds like a good argument for staying off trains, perhaps for keeping to your cars instead. But

when you look at the figure more closely, you learn that it means something quite different. Nearly half of the victims were people whose cars ran into trains at crossings. Only one hundred and thirty-two were passengers on trains.

(Words 73)

4. According to the passage, which of the following statements is true?

A) People should keep away from the train.

B) More people on trains are killed each year than those in cars.

C) People should avoid travelling by train and by car.

D) Travelling by train is relatively safe.

Section II Passage Two

Becoming a Mortgage Slave or Not

Housing prices are keeping rising, especially in many parts of the country. Hesitating to buy a house means that you will never afford to buy your own house in the future. So the post-1980s struggle to buy their first one. They believe that it may be an affordable time for them to buy their first house, considering the job stability, the desire to settle down, and the low interest rates for the first-time buyers. Nowadays the interest rates are pretty much lower. Nobody knows whether this favourable financial policy will be changed or not. Besides, most people have the strong desire to settle down. For those people who have strong career stability and can afford to pay the monthly mortgage, buying a house on mortgage is a feasible option. So, if your career is stable, and you are satisfied with your present situation, buying a house becomes a more attractive option.

But a lot of uncertainty about the housing market and the economy still remains. You should think about it carefully. Although a monthly mortgage payment may be comparable in some cases to a monthly rent, there are other expenses to consider. The post-80s are still getting a grasp on their future and have a constant change of lifestyle. The housing price is so high that life is hard for most people who earn just enough to pay their mortgage. They will take a very heavy financial burden, as they have to pay their mortgage monthly. The costs for buying a house could add up to about 6% of the sale price, or roughly two or three years' worth of rents. Renting a house makes it possible to lead a comfortable life.

In conclusion, everyone has different choices about becoming a mortgage slave.

(Words 304)

（节选自《英语畅谈流行时尚 50 主题》）

New Words（★三级词汇 ◆超纲词汇）

◆ mortgage ['mɔːgɪdʒ]   *v.* 按揭（由银行等提供房产抵押借款）
　 hesitate ['hezɪteɪt]   *v.* 犹豫；（对某事）迟疑不决
　 affordable [ə'fɔːdəbl]   *a.* 付得起的；买得起的
◆ stability [stə'bɪlətɪ]   *n.* 稳定（性）；稳固（性）
　 favourable ['feɪvərəbl]   *a.* 给人好印象的；赞同的
★ financial [faɪ'nænʃl]   *a.* 财政的；财务的
★ career [kə'rɪə(r)]   *n.* 生涯；职业
★ feasible ['fiːzəbl]   *a.* 可行的；行得通的
　 option ['ɒpʃn]   *n.* 可选择的事物；选择；选择权
　 stable ['steɪbl]   *a.* 稳定的；稳固的
　 uncertainty [ʌn'sɜːtntɪ]   *n.* 犹豫；迟疑
　 economy [ɪ'kɒnəmɪ]   *n.* 经济；经济情况；经济结构
　 payment ['peɪmənt]   *n.* 付款；支付
★ comparable ['kɒmpərəbl]   *a.* 类似的；可比较的
　 expense [ɪk'spens]   *n.* 费用；价钱
　 burden ['bɜːdn]   *n.* （义务、责任等的）重担；负担
　　　　　　　　　　　　 v. （使）担负（沉重或艰难的任务、职责等）
　 roughly ['rʌflɪ]   *ad.* 大约；大致
　 conclusion [kən'kluːʒn]   *n.* 结论；推论

Phrases and Expressions

hesitate to do sth. 做某事迟疑
afford to do 支付得起；（买）得起（某物）
settle down 定居，过安定生活
interest rate 利率；利息

be satisfied with 对……感到满意

in some cases 在一些情况下

add up to 总计达；意味着

in conclusion 最后，总之

Read and Choose

V. There are five questions or unfinished statements in the following. For each of them there are four choices marked A, B, C and D. Choose the best answer according to Passage Two.

1. People think they shouldn't hesitate to buy a house, because_____.

   A) housing prices are keeping rising

   B) people want to buy a house

   C) people have money to buy a house

   D) people have time to buy a house

2. According to the passage, which of the following statements is not true?

   A) The post-1980s struggle to buy their first house.

   B) This favorable financial policy will not be changed in the future.

   C) The interest rates are pretty much lower.

   D) Most people have the strong desire to settle down.

3. For some people, buying a house becomes a more attractive option. Which statement is not the real reason?

   A) Because they have strong career stability.

   B) Because they can afford to pay the monthly mortgage.

   C) Because they are satisfied with their present situation.

   D) Because they can borrow enough money from parents.

4. What can we learn from the passage?

   A) Buying a house is easy for young people.

   B) Most people do not buy their first house.

   C) Buying a house is difficult for young people.

   D) Renting a house is a good idea for all people.

5. What is the author's attitude about buying a house now?

   A) Supporting.

   B) Cautious.

   C) Opposing.

   D) Not mentioned.

Unit One　Social Issues

VI. In this part, there are five sentences (the first four are taken from the two passages). Below each, there are five Chinese sentences translated, which marked A, B, C, D and E. You should decide which is the best translation.

1. If they spend a long time testing the affection, it's just to put obstacles on their own way. *(Passage One)*
   A. 如果用一段时间去测试是否有感情，就是在自找麻烦。
   B. 如果用时间的长短去衡量能否吃苦，那他们就在回家的路上了。
   C. 如果再花费大量的时间去验证爱情，就是给自己设置障碍。
   D. 如果他们用时间去测试友情，那就是想给自己找麻烦。
   E. 如果他们花费很长时间考验感情，那就是在自找麻烦。

2. If the affection can't go on forever, both sides will be deeply hurt and no one can relive their past youth. *(Passage One)*
   A. 如果双方受了伤之后，感受就不可能继续下去了，谁都不会回来买青春了。
   B. 一旦爱情无法永远延续下去了，双方都会受伤不说，没人做得到回味过去。
   C. 感情一旦无法继续走下去，两方都会受伤，而且没人把你的青春还给你。
   D. 感受如果无法继续，谁又能够为受伤的人们买回你们的青春岁月呢？
   E. 如果爱情走不下去了，双方受伤不说，也没有人可以为消逝的青春"买单"。

3. They believe that it may be an affordable time for them to buy their first house, considering the job stability, the desire to settle down, and the low interest rates for the first-time buyers. *(Passage Two)*
   A. 他们相信他们的第一套房就时间来说是可购买的，如果工作固定了，银行利率又很低，他们就可以考虑安定下来的事情了。
   B. 他们相信可能是因为工作固定下来了，安定下来以后银行的利率就会很低的，所以这是买房的好时候。
   C. 考虑到两人工作稳定，希望安定下来，况且初次购房者也可以享受较低的贷款利率，所以他们认为是购买首套住房的好时机了。
   D. 银行相信，假若他们工作固定以后，买房子的利率就会因为工作固定而给予优惠条件，那就是银行给他们很低的利息。
   E. 他们考虑到两个人工作稳定，可以享受利率较低的银行贷款，所以希望到了对他们来说可以支付第一套住房的费用的时间了。

4. Although a monthly mortgage payment may be comparable in some cases to a monthly rent, there are other expenses to consider. *(Passage Two)*
   A. 尽管月供跟你租房的费用相比较，仍然还有其他的某些费用要考虑支出。
   B. 虽然，月供和房租的费用也差不了多少，但除了月供你还得支出其他费用。

13

C. 虽然月供在有些情况下可以跟你一个月租房的费用对比，但还要考虑其他费用。

D. 虽然有些情况下，月供跟你每月租房的费用差不多，不过还得考虑其他开支。

E. 月供跟在你租房的以外要考虑的其他的费用相比较，仍然有特殊情况。

5. Understanding your own personality is an important step in knowing how you relate to the world and those who are around you.

   A. 了解自己的个性，就知道与人打交道的重要的一步了。

   B. 了解自己的个性，在知道怎么与世界和你周围的人打交道是重要的。

   C. 了解自己的性格，对如何待人接物有非常重要的帮助。

   D. 了解自己的性格，在怎样打交道方面是重要的。

   E. 了解自己的个性的重要的阶段，就是与世界有关。

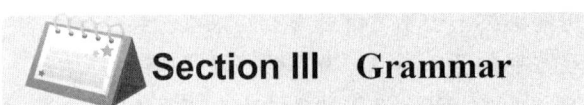

Section III　Grammar

Infinitive（不定式）

　　动词不定式指由 to 加上动词原形（而且只能是动词原形）所构成的一种非限定性动词，但在有些情况下 to 可以省略。动词不定式在语法功能上可作主语、宾语、表语、定语和状语。

　　动词不定式仍具有动词的属性，所以动词不定式及其短语还可以有自己的宾语、状语，虽然动词不定式在语法上没有表面上的直接主语，但它表达的意义是动作，这一动作一定由使动者发出，这一使动者我们称之为逻辑主语。

Review and Practice

VII. There are 10 incomplete sentences below. For each one, there are four choices marked A, B, C and D. You should choose the best answer.

1. The chair looks rather hard, but in fact it is very comfortable _____.

   A) to sit　　　　　B) to sit on　　　　C) to be seat　　　D) to be sat on

2. Paul doesn't have to be made _____. He always works hard.

   A) learn　　　　　B) to learn　　　　C) learned　　　　D) learning

3. She pretended _____ me when I passed by.

   A) not to see　　　B) not seeing　　　C) to not see　　　D) having not seen

4. The boy wanted to ride his bicycle in the street, but his mother told him _____.

	A) not to	B) not to do	C) not do it	D) do not to

5. —I usually go there by train.
   —Why not _____ by boat for a change?
   A) to try going   B) trying to go   C) to try and go   D) try going

6. —The light in the office is still on.
   —Oh, I forgot _____.
   A) turning it off   B) turn it off   C) to turn it off   D) having turned it off

7. She reached the top of the hill and stopped _____ on a big rock by the side of the path.
   A) to have rested   B) resting   C) to rest   D) rest

8. I find _____ to answer all the questions within the time given.
   A) no possibility   B) there was impossibility
   C) impossible   D) it impossible

9. They knew her very well. They had seen her _____ up from childhood.
   A) grow   B) grew   C) was growing   D) to grow

10. The bank is reported in the local newspaper _____ the day before yesterday.
    A) to have been robbed   B) robbed
    C) having been robbed   D) to rob

VIII. Put the proper forms of the following words in the blanks to complete the sentences.

1. The boy was made _____ (sing) the song once again.
2. There was nothing to do except _____ (escape).
3. They would rather _____ (die) than _____ (surrender).
4. I have no idea of how _____ (do) it.
5. The problem is said _____ (discuss) three times.

Section IV Writing

Invitation Card/ Letter（请柬）

Invitation card/ letter for personal situations almost always involves one person inviting another/others to a social function. For most of these events (e.g. weddings, parties, baptisms, etc.), ready-made, pre-printed invitations can be purchased at stationery stores, eliminating the need to specifically write personal invitation letters for most of these situations.

Sample 1

Mr.& Mrs. Steve Johnson
request the pleasure of the company of
Mr. & Mrs. Arthur Smith
On the occasion of the marriage of their daughter
Sandra
to
Mr.Martin Quinn
in the
church of the Immaculate Conception
Racheen
On Saturday, 4th October, 2014
at 2 p.m.
and afterwards at a reception in
the Court Hotel, Racheen
94 Marbell Road, Racheen
Co. Dublin

- R.S.V.P.
- By 1st October
- Tel. 8123456

Sample 2

100 Zizhu Road
Beijing,100083
March 1st, 2015

Dear Prof. Smith,

    My wife and I would be very happy if you could come to dinner on Sunday, March 8th, at 6:30 in the evening. We are having a party at Tianyuan Hotel. We do hope you can join us.

Sincerely yours
Albert Shaw

IX. Write an invitation card.

    格林先生及夫人：兹订于2015年1月3日（星期六）下午三时半，在纽约天安教堂为小女玛丽·史密斯与乔治·布朗先生举办结婚典礼。敬请光临！

约翰·史密斯夫妇

Section V　Enjoy Yourselves

A Song

Need You Now

-Lady Antebellum

Picture perfect memories scattered all around the floor
Reaching for the phone'cause I can't fight it anymore
And I wonder if I ever cross your mind
For me it happens all the time
It's a quarter after one, I'm all alone and I need you now
Said I wouldn't call but I lost all control and I need you now
And I don't know how I can do without, I just need you now
Another shot of whiskey can't stop looking at the door
Wishing you'd come sweeping in the way you did before
And I wonder if I ever cross your mind
For me it happens all the time
It's a quarter after one I'm a little drunk and I need you now
Said I wouldn't call but I lost all control and I need you now
And I don't know how I can do without I just need you now
Ooh...
Guess I'd rather hurt than feel nothing at all
It's a quarter after one I'm all alone and I need you now
And I said I wouldn't call but I'm a little drunk and I need you now
And I don't know how I can do without I just need you now
I just need you now
Oh baby I need you now

Unit Two Life Experience

➢ Warm-up Question

Do you have any special life experiences that have deep impact on your life?

Section I Listening & Speaking

◆ **Listening**

Task 1.

Directions: In this section, you will hear 6 short conversations. At the end of each conversation, a question will be asked about what was said. Both the conversation and the question will be spoken twice. After each question there will be a pause. During the pause you must read the four choices marked A), B), C) and D), and decide which is the best answer. Then mark your answer.

Example:
You will hear:
M: Is it possible for you to work late, Miss Green?
W: Work late? I suppose so, if you really think it's necessary.
Q: Where does the conversation most probably take place?

You will read:
A) At the office.
B) In the waiting room.
C) At the airport.
D) In a restaurant.

Unit Two   Life Experience

From the conversation we know that the two were talking about some work they had to finish in the evening. This is most likely to have taken place at the office. Therefore, A) "At the office" is the best answer. You should choose answer A).

Sample Answer

A)   B)   C)   D)

Now let us listen to 6 short conversations, both the conversation and the question will be spoken twice.

1. A) Two years.   B) Three months.
    C) Four weeks.   D) Five years.
2. A) She'll go to the theatre.   B) She'll go to Kunming.
    C) She'll drive to see her sister.   D) She'll drive her mother to the airport.
3. A) It's not important how he dances.   B) It's too crowded to dance away.
    C) If he's careful, no one will notice.   D) No one knows the steps of dance.
4. A) Doctor and patient.   B) Teacher and student.
    C) Shop assistant and customer.   D) Boss and clerk.
5. A) At an art gallery.   B) In a department store.
    C) At a bookstore.   D) In a workshop.
6. A) One dollar.   B) Two dollars.
    C) Three dollars.   D) Four dollars.

Task 2.

Directions: In this section, you will hear a short passage. At the end of the passage, you will hear two questions. Both the passage and the questions will be spoken twice. After you hear One question, you must choose the best answer from the four choices marked A), B), C) and D). Then mark your answer.

1. A) When they are old.
    B) When they can't see perfectly.
    C) When they go to see a doctor.
    D) When they can see well.
2. A) They can't see close things clearly.
    B) They have to wear glasses.
    C) They can see things that are far away.
    D) They can't read books.

Task 3.

A. **Directions:** In this section, you will hear a passage three times. Listen carefully during the first reading. Then listen to the passage again. When it is being read the second times, you should fill in the ten blanks numbered from S1) to S10) with the exact words or phrases you have just heard. Finally, when the passage is read for the third time, you should check what you have written.

New Words and Expressions

commit suicide 自杀

◆spur [spɜ:] *n.* 刺激，鼓舞

★estimate ['estɪmeɪt] *v.* 估计，估价，判断

Larry Smith is one of the **S1)** _____ on the Golden Gate Bridge. His job is to save people who **S2)** _____ to jump into the sea. If the telephone rings at three in the morning, he knows it's trouble. Someone is **S3)** _____ to commit suicide. Larry will get his things ready and in no time he will be out of the door **S4)** _____ to the **S5)** _____. Many suicide attempts are made on the spur of the moment and lives can be saved. But if he fails, if the person jumps into the **S6)** _____ pool, there's no **S7)** _____ how helpless he feels. The **S8)** _____ is to open a **S9)** _____ of communication with them. Following is one trick that has worked. "Hey, if you're going to jump, at least give me your mum's phone number. So I can call and tell her." Sometimes all it works is the voice of the human being who cares. Larry **S10)** _____ he has rescued 38 people in his ten years of service.

B. Listen to the passage again and then decide whether each of the following statements is true (T) or false (F).

1. (   ) When the telephone rings at three in the morning, Larry will not go to the spot.
2. (   ) The trick to save people is to stop them from jumping.
3. (   ) Sometimes the voice of the human being who cares can work.
4. (   ) Larry has been doing this work for many years.

◆ **Speaking**

Task 1. Talk about one life experience that has deep impression on you.

Task 2. Two students are in a pair to make a conversation as the following sample.

Unit Two　Life Experience

Bill:　Hi, Sam!
Sam:　Hi, Bill! Can you come to my birthday party next Sunday?
Bill:　Thanks for your invitation. I'd love to come.
Sam:　Great! A lot of friends will come.
Bill:　Who else have you asked?
Sam:　Kate, Ann, Jack, Bruce and the twins.
Bill:　What time is it going to start?
Sam:　About half past four.
Bill:　OK. But I'm afraid I may be a little later. I must finish my homework first.
Sam:　It doesn't matter.
Bill:　Ok. Then see you!
Sam:　See you!

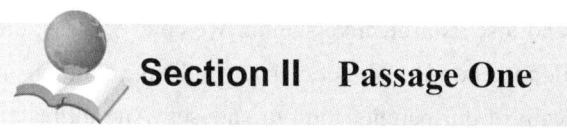

Section II　Passage One

The Art of Living

　　The art of living is to know when to hold fast and when to let go. For life is a paradox: it instructs us to cling to its many gifts even while it ordains their eventual giving up.

　　Surely we ought to hold fast to life, for it is marvelous, and full of beauty that breaks through every pore of God's own earth. We know that this is so, but all too often we recognize this truth only in our backward glance when we remember what was and then suddenly realize that it is no more.

　　A recent experience re-taught me this truth. I was hospitalized following a severe heart attack and had been in intensive care for several days. It was not a pleasant place.

One morning, I had to have some additional tests. The required machines were located in a building at the opposite end of the hospital, so I had to be wheeled across the courtyard on a gurney.

As we emerged from our unit, the sunlight hit me. That's all there was to my experience, just the light of the sun. And yet how beautiful it was—how warm, how sparkling, how brilliant! I looked to see whether anyone else appreciated the sun's golden glow, but everyone was hurrying to and fro, most with eyes fixed on the ground. Then I remembered how often I, too, had been indifferent to the grandeur of each day, too preoccupied with petty and sometimes even mean concerns to respond to the splendor of it all.

The insight got from that experience is really as commonplace as was the experience itself: life's gifts are precious—but we are too careless of them.

At every stage of life we suffer losses—and grow in the process. We begin our independent lives only when we emerge from the womb and lose its protective shelter. We enter schools, then we leave our mothers and fathers and our childhood homes. We get married and have children and then have to let them go. We confront the death of our parents and our spouses. And ultimately, we must confront the inevitability of our own death, losing ourselves as it were, all that we were or dreamed to be.

(Words 381)

（Excerpted from *English Salon*, by John Boynton Priestley）

New Words（★三级词汇 ◆超纲词汇）

◆paradox ['pærədɒks]　*n.* 矛盾的人（或事物、情况）

　instruct [ɪn'strʌkt]　*v.* 指示，命令，吩咐

◆cling [klɪŋ]　*v.* 抓紧，紧握，紧抱

◆ordain [ɔː'deɪn]　*v.* 主宰，掌握，注定

★eventual [ɪ'ventʃuːəl]　*a.* 最终的，最后的

★marvelous ['mɑːvələs]　*a.* 极好的，非凡的

◆pore [pɔː(r)]　*n.* 毛孔，气孔，细孔

　recognize ['rekəgnaɪz]　*v.* 认识，认出，辨别出

　glance [glɑːns]　*n.* 匆匆一看，一瞥，扫视

★hospitalize ['hɒspɪtəlaɪz]　*v.* 送（某人）入院治疗

★severe [sɪ'vɪə(r)]　*a.* 极为恶劣的，十分严重的

　intensive [ɪn'tensɪv]　*a.* 密集的；彻底的；十分细致的

Unit Two Life Experience

★additional [əˈdɪʃənl]   *a.* 外加的，附加的，额外的
◆gurney [gɜːnɪ]   *n.* （医院中推送病人用的）轮床
  emerge [ɪˈmɜːdʒ]   *v.* 出现，浮现，露出

◆sparkling [spɑːklɪŋ]   *a.* 闪烁的，闪耀的
  brilliant [ˈbrɪljənt]   *a.* 印象深刻的，闪光的，辉煌的
  appreciate [əˈprɪʃɪeɪt]   *v.* 感激，感谢，欣赏
  indifferent [ɪnˈdɪfrənt]   *a.* 漠不关心的，不感兴趣的

◆grandeur [ˈɡrændʒə(r)]   *n.* 宏伟，壮丽，堂皇
★preoccupy [prɪˈɒkjupaɪ]   *v.* 使日夜思考，使忧心忡忡
◆petty [ˈpetɪ]   *a.* 小的，琐碎的，不重要的
  precious [ˈpreʃəs]   *a.* 珍奇的，宝贵的，珍贵的
★insight [ˈɪnsaɪt]   *n.* 洞察力；领悟
  commonplace [ˈkɒmənpleɪs]   *n.* 寻常的事物，平常的东西
◆womb [wuːm]   *n.* 子宫
◆spouse [spaus]   *n.* 配偶；夫或妻
★confront [kənˈfrʌnt]   *v.* 面对；处理；解决
★ultimately [ˈʌltɪmətlɪ]   *ad.* 最终，最后，终归
★inevitability [ɪnˌevɪtəˈbɪlətɪ]   *n.* 必然性

Phrases and Expressions

  let go   放开；释放；发射
  give up   放弃；放手
◆cling to   保留；紧抓；坚持
  all too often   时常
  break through   突围；突破
  no more   不再
  be located in   坐落于，位于
  to and fro   来回地；往复地

Read and Think

I. Answer the following questions according to the passage.

1. What is the art of living according to the author?
2. What re-taught me the art of living?
3. When do we begin our independent lives?

Read and Try

II. Fill in each blank with a right word in its right form using the words in the following box.

| ultimately | instruct | severe | emerge |
| additional | intensive | precious | marvelous |

1. There we received several weeks of _____ training.
2. An excess of rain caused _____ floods.
3. Pandas are _____ creatures.
4. _____, the President makes all decisions.
5. Their performance was _____.
6. The teacher _____ the students to work on their pronunciation.
7. We needed _____ money for our trip.
8. Suddenly, the boss _____ from his office.

III. There are eight incomplete sentences below. For each sentence, there are four choices marked A, B, C and D. You should choose the proper one to complete each sentence.

1. Some people still cling _____ the old customs and beliefs.
   A) with   B) for
   C) to   D) by
2. You must _____ your problems.
   A) offense   B) confront
   C) challenge   D) glance
3. Positive signs are beginning to _____.
   A) face   B) apparent
   C) break   D) emerge
4. Does he need to _____?
   A) be hospitalized   B) hospitalized
   C) be hospitalize   D) hospitalize
5. He sat there, with his eyes _____.
   A) close   B) closing
   C) closed   D) being closed
6. The six blind men stood there, _____ for a meal.
   A) beg   B) begged
   C) were begging   D) begging

7. _____ by the house, he saw a girl playing the piano.
   A) Pass B) Passing
   C) Passed D) Having passed
8. Don't be angry with me for _____ written to you.
   A) not having B) having not
   C) not have D) have not

Read and Translate

IV. Translate the following sentences into English.
1. 他不想放过任何练习英语的机会。(let go)
2. 坚持过时的观点和理论是很危险的。(cling to)
3. 他们发现难以突围成功，只得逃跑了。(break through)
4. 他显得很紧张，身体不停地前后摇摆。(to and fro)

Reading Skills

General Idea

When you are reading, you must understand the article's general idea. To find a passage's main idea, you can use the reading skills of skimming. Usually there is one sentence to express the whole article's general idea or the topic. This sentence may appear in the first paragraph or in the last paragraph or in the middle of the article. However, sometimes there may not be such a stated topic sentence. In that case, the main idea is hinted but not stated outright.

I. Directions: Give the title of the following paragraphs.

Passage One

Forests are very important to people. People get wood for fuel and lumber for houses in the forests. They get food from the plant and trees. They also get other things like rubber, wax, rattan and bamboo from the forests.

(Words 40)

Passage Two

Isabel seldom misses her daily mess. Everybody loves her because she talks softly. She never utters hurting words to anybody. Her friends say she is a very religious and kind girl.

(Words 31)

II. Directions: Write down the general idea of the following passages.

Passage Three

Of all the essential nutrients, water is the most important. One can survive on the body's stored food for as long as ten weeks but without water, life would be over in a few days.

(Words 35)

Passage Four

After three day's travel through space, Apollo 11 reached the moon's orbit. Astronauts Neil Armstrong and Edwin Aldrin climbed into the Eagle, a human module designed to take them from the spaceship and land on the moon. On July 20, 1969, Armstrong and Aldrin were the first people to walk on the moon.

(Words 53)

Section II   Passage Two

7 Ways to Find Out What You Really Want in Life

Be Selfish

You can't pinpoint exactly what you want in life if you're constantly sacrificing your time and dreams for other people. You have to put yourself first. Ask yourself: if you weren't tied down by your job, family, friends, or anything else, then what would you be doing right now? Always remember that it's okay to put yourself first, because if you don't, then no one else will.

Regret Nothing

Don't feel bad for being selfish. It's your life. It's time for you to live it exactly the way you want to. If you constantly regret things you did or didn't do in the past, then you won't be able to move forward. Don't live in the past. Live in the present…and the future!

Figure Out What You Need

Sometimes it's hard to figure out what you need. Sit down and think about what you need the most. Is it your family? Love? Financial security? If it helps, you can make a list of priorities. Also think about the kind of legacy you want to leave behind.

Determine What Really Bothers You

You can soar only by pushing back against something you don't want. Figure out what upsets you. Don't just say that you hate your office job. Pinpoint exactly why you hate it. Could it be your micromanaging boss? What bothers you, and how can you fix it? How much do you want to fix it?

Determine What Makes You Truly Happy

Your happiness is the root of your desires. So take a few moments and really think about what makes you happy. Is it traveling? Being around children? Financial freedom? Once you pinpoint the one thing that makes you happy most, you'll have a pretty clear idea of what you should strive for in your life.

Let People Around You Know What You're Trying to Achieve

Don't keep your goals and desires to yourself. Voice it all out! If you tell people what you're trying to accomplish, they will most likely support you and give you new ideas. Sometimes mother does know best!

Stay Positive

Life doesn't always go how you want it. Don't feel dismay as your plans stray. Take control. Instead of freaking out, try your best to roll with the changes. You will get there someday. You're just taking a little detour. Sometimes a positive attitude is all you need to keep going.

(Words 399)

(Excerpted from: China Daily.com.cn, iNews)

New Words（★三级词汇　◆超纲词汇）

◆pinpoint [ˈpɪnpɔɪnt]　v. 确定，准确地指出；精准定位

★sacrifice [ˈsækrɪfaɪs]　v. 牺牲，把……奉献给……；廉价卖出；牺牲，献祭

★financial [faɪnænʃl]　a. 财政的，金融的

★priority [praɪˈɒrətɪ]　n. 优先，在前

◆legacy [ˈlegəsɪ]　n. 遗产，遗赠；遗留问题；后遗

◆strive [straɪv]　v. 努力奋斗，力求；斗争，力争

★accomplish [əˈkʌmplɪʃ]　v. 完成，实现

◆stray [streɪ]　v. 走失；偏离正题；走入歧途；（已婚者或有固定关系者）有外遇

◆dismay [dɪsˈmeɪ]　n. 沮丧；绝望

　　　　　　　　　　v. 使……沮丧；使……绝望

　roll [rəʊl]　v. 滚动，滚落，翻落；使摇摆，使摇晃；碾；绕，卷

　　　　　　　n. 一卷，卷状物；面包卷；名单，名册

◆detour [ˈdiːtʊə(r)]　n. 绕路，绕道

Phrases and Expressions

figure out　计算出，弄明白，解决，合计
push back　推出；使撤退，使回到原处
voice it all out　大声说出来

freak out 疯狂、兴奋的感受（尤指因毒品所致）

Read and Choose

V. There are five questions or unfinished statements in the following. For each of them there are four choices marked A, B, C and D. Decide the best answer according to Passage Two.

1. This passage mainly talks about _____.
   A) some ways to find out what you really want in life
   B) we should be selfish in our life
   C) how to do well in our life
   D) finding out what you really want in life

2. Which of the following does not belong to the ways?
   A) Be selfish.   B) Stay positive.
   C) Regret nothing.   D) Open your mind.

3. How can you figure out what you need according to the author?
   A) Just sit down.   B) Only think about.
   C) Sit down and think about. D) Take a rest.

4. According to the author, how many ways are there to find out what you really want in life?
   A) 6.   B) 7.   C) 5.   D) 8.

5. "Micromanaging" in paragraph 8 means_____?
   A) 微软   B) 微小管理   C) 细，严   D) 管理

VI. In this part, there are five sentences (the first four are taken from the two passages). Below each, there are five Chinese sentences translated, which marked A, B, C, D and E. You should decide which is the best translation.

1. The insight got from that experience is really as commonplace as was the experience itself. *(Passage One)*
   A) 从那次经历中吸取的认识与那次经历本身一样极为寻常。
   B) 那次经历就像一个普通的地方一样，带给我的体验也是很普通的。
   C) 从那次经历中得到的认识与那次经历本身一样极为寻常。
   D) 从那次经历中领悟的认识与那次经历的事情一样极为常见。
   E) 与以往的经历相比，这次的经历给我的启发是一样的。

2. And ultimately, we must confront the inevitability of our own death, losing ourselves as it were, all that we were or dreamed to be. *(Passage One)*

A) 最后，我们必须直面我们自己无法逃避的死亡，失去原来的方向，失去我们所有的一切或者我们所梦想的一切。

B) 最终我们必须不可避免地死亡，失去自己，离开自己的世界，我们的梦想和拥有的一切也会随之烟消云散。

C) 最后，我们不可避免地都要死去，失去自我，要离开这个世界，带走我们以前所拥有的一切和曾经拥有的梦想。

D) 最后，我们必须面对我们自己不可避免的死亡，失去原本的自己，失去我们所有的一切或者我们所梦想的一切。

E) 最终，我们必须被死亡不可避免地征服，带着所有的一切和梦想而迷失在这个世界里，同时失去自己的方向。

3. You can't pinpoint exactly what you want in life if you're constantly sacrificing your time and dreams for other people. *(Passage Two)*

   A) 如果你一直是为了别人而牺牲自己的时间和梦想，那你就不能精确地定位你到底想在生活中得到什么。

   B) 你不能准确定位你想要的是什么样的生活，如果你不断地牺牲自己的时间和梦想而为别人。

   C) 你不能准确指出你到底想要什么，假如你不断地牺牲自己的时间和梦想。

   D) 假如你不断地浪费你的时间和梦想，你就不能准确指出你想要什么。

   E) 如果你一直为了别人浪费你的梦想和时间，你就不能准确定位你到底在生活中想得到什么。

4. You can soar only by pushing back against something you don't want. *(Passage Two)*

   A) 只有在推走那些你不想要的东西后，你才能高飞。

   B) 你可以翱翔，只要抵制一些你不想要的东西。

   C) 你可以反推回去一些你不想要的东西，这样你就能飞。

   D) 你要升高，可以通过丢弃一些你不想要的东西。

   E) 你可以高飞，只有排除一些你不想要的东西。

5. Given his lack of experience, his work is remarkably good.

   A) 他的工作非常出色，虽然没什么经验。

   B) 他的工作非常出色，但是他没有经验。

   C) 如果他没有工作经验，他的表现非常出色。

   D) 已经给了他一次经验，他的工作非常出色。

   E) 即使他缺乏经验，他的工作也非常引人注目。

Section III　Grammar

Participle（分词）

分词（participle）也是一种非限定性动词。有现在分词（present participle）和过去分词（past participle）两种。现在分词在动词原形后加后缀-ing 构成，过去分词一般形式在动词原形加后缀-ed 构成。分词在句子中可作表语、定语、状语、补语等。分词也可有其独立的逻辑主语。这种主语常常是名词或代词主格，置于分词之前，二者构成一种分词独立结构。

Review and Practice

VII. There are 10 incomplete sentences below. For each one, there are four choices marked A, B, C and D. You should choose the best answer.

1. Anyone _____ bags, boxes, or whatever, was stopped by the police.
   A) seen carry   B) seen carrying
   C) saw to carry   D) saw carrying

2. The plane crashed _____ all 200 people aboard.
   A) killed   B) having killed
   C) killing   D) had killed

3. We solved the problem by reducing our costs and _____ more money.
   A) borrowed   B) borrowing
   C) would borrow   D) had borrow

4. _____ all this, they made me pay for the damage.
   A) Knowing   B) Knew
   C) To know   D) Having know

5. The new manager came to our company last week, _____ with him plenty of new ideas.
   A) bringing   B) brought
   C) to bring   D) to have brought

6. Any student _____ will be disqualified from the exam.
   A) catching cheating   B) catching to cheat
   C) caught cheating   D) caught to cheat

7. She always reads the letter through before sending it, _____ for spelling mistakes.
   A) checked   B) to be checking
   C) checking   D) having checked

Unit Two Life Experience

8. Never touch an electric wire when it is _____.
   A) broken   B) break
   C) breaking   D) to break
9. He sat in the armchair, _____ the newspaper.
   A) read   B) to read
   C) reading   D) having read
10. The dark clouds _____, the sun shone again.
    A) having disappeared   B) disappearing
    C) had disappeared   D) having disappearing

VIII. Put the proper forms of the following words in the blanks to complete the sentences.

1. It was a windy day, and the air _____ (stir) on Dorrit's face soon brightened it.
2. He had been a pioneer in California, and could narrate many a strange tale of fortunes (make)_____ and fortunes _____ (lose) in those wild halcyon days.
3. My two _____ (grow) children have both finished college.
4. Dick jumped out of the way of the _____ (approach) train.
5. Her husband was a _____ (retire) tradesman.

Section IV Writing

Business Card（名片）

A small card printed with one's name, professional occupation, company position, business address, and other contact information.

Sample

> China International Import-Export Company
> Wang Tianwang   General Manager
> Address: No.36 Lane 1122 Beijing Road
> Home Phone: (021)8459993   Office Phone: (021)82450331
> Zip Code: 201104   E-mail: wang2005@sina.com.cn

IX. Translate the following business cards into English.

吉林省水利厅

赵鸿儒　局长

地址：中国长春市人民大街 48 号
邮编：130051　电话 0431－2714465　0431－5604793（宅）

Section V　Enjoy Yourselves

Funny Pictures

Square Watermelon, Grown in Boxes

Wedding in a Truck

Sleeping While Eating

Pet Holder

Unit Three   Environment

➤ Warm-up Question

What is the situation of environmental protection in China?

Section I   Listening & Speaking

◆ Listening

Task 1.

Directions: In this section, you will hear 6 short conversations. At the end of each conversation, a question will be asked about what was said. Both the conversation and the question will be spoken twice. After each question there will be a pause. During the pause you must read the four choices marked A), B), C) and D), and decide which is the best answer. Then mark your answer.

Example:

You will hear:

M: Is it possible for you to work late, Miss Green?

W: Work late? I suppose so, if you really think it's necessary.

Q: Where does the conversation most probably take place?

You will read:

A) At the office.
B) In the waiting room.
C) At the airport.
D) In a restaurant.

From the conversation we know that they two were talking about some work they had to finish in the evening. This is most likely to have taken place at the office. Therefore, A) "At the office" is the best answer. You should choose answer A).

Sample Answer

A)   B)   C)   D)

New Words and Expressions

◆intolerable [ɪnˈtɒlərəbl]   *a.* 无法忍受的，难耐的

destruction [dɪˈstrʌkʃn]   *n.* 破坏，毁灭

◆bacteria [bækˈtɪərɪə]   *n.*（pl.）（复数）细菌

◆SARS 非典型肺炎 （Severe Acute Respiratory Syndrome）

bird flu [bɜːd ˈfluː] 禽流感

be aware of 察觉到；意识到；发觉；发现

Now let us listen to 6 short conversations, both the conversation and the question will be spoken twice.

1. A) How to make use of the time in our daily life.
   B) How to reduce waste in our daily life.
   C) How to do that exercise.
   D) How to clean up the classroom.

2. A) They don't know SARS.
   B) They haven't realized the environmental destruction.
   C) Lucy doesn't agree with Tom.
   D) They are talking about environment pollution.

3. A) It may pollute the air.
   B) It doesn't pollute our environment.
   C) It may pollute the water.
   D) It may pollute the places we live in.

4. A) Because there are many cars on the road.
   B) Because many people make the noise on the street.
   C) Because the factory has been producing cars for a long time.
   D) Because the road near his house has been mended for more than half a year, and it is still not completed.

5. A) The environmental pollution.   B) The world problem.

C) The problem around us. D) The problem in China.
6. A) Using certain types of drugs. B) Using certain types of bacteria.
C) Using certain types of medicine. D) Using certain types of ways.

Task 2. Listening Comprehension

Directions: In this section, you will hear a short passage. At the end of the passage, you will hear two questions. Both the passage and the questions will be spoken twice. After you hear a question, you must choose the best answer from the four choices marked A), B), C) and D). Then mark your answer.

New Words and Expressions

release [rɪˈliːs] v. 释放，发射
◆respiratory [rəˈspɪrətrɪ] a. 呼吸的，与呼吸有关的
garbage [ˈgɑːbɪdʒ] n. 垃圾，废物，食物残渣
spoil [spɔɪl] v. 破坏，腐坏
splendid [ˈsplendɪd] a. 极好的，辉煌的，壮观的，杰出的
deserve [dɪˈzɜːv] v. 应受，值得

1. A) One factor of pollution is that people throw their garbage everywhere.
   B) People are encouraged to use paper products.
   C) People don't pay attention to the industrial pollution.
   D Transportation is the main factor of pollution.
2. A) People are encouraged to use more plastic products.
   B) People classify the garbage and some is recycled after being collected.
   C) People begin to buy cars to prevent pollution.
   D) The greenhouse effect problem has been solved.

Task 3.

A. **Directions:** In this section, you will hear a passage three times. Listen carefully during the first reading. Then listen to the passage again. When it is being read the second time, you should fill in the ten blanks numbered from S1) to S10) with the exact words or phrases you have just heard. Finally, when the passage is read for the third time, you should check what you have written.

New Words and Expressions

◆poisonous ['pɔɪzənəs]   *a.* 引起中毒的；有毒的
◆disable [dɪs'eɪbl]   *v.* 使……失去能力
★significance [sɪg'nɪfɪkəns]   *n.* 重要性，意义
★household ['haʊshəʊld]   *n.* 家庭，户
  be responsible for   对……负责，对……有责任

Most of us today **S1)** _____ that environmental pollution has been a greatly serious problem. Lots of plants, trees and crops are **S2)** _____ by bad air. Many fish die of **S3)** _____. Thousands of people die from eating poisoned fish and breathing in gas. Therefore, **S4)** _____ should be responsible for these diseases that are **S5)** _____, or bringing death not only to human beings, but also to wild lives. The **S6)** _____ for controlling pollution noted that it's high time that more effective **S7)** _____ should be taken. Therefore, new laws should be passed to limit the amount of **S8)** _____ from factories. Moreover, in the households, there is an obvious need to **S9)** _____ litter and waste. Let's make our good efforts, and the world will be a **S10)** _____ place to live for us.

B. Listen to the passage again and then decide whether each of the following statements is true (T) or false (F).

1. (   ) Most of us today have recognized that environmental pollution has been a greatly serious problem.
2. (   ) Environmental pollution is only responsible for human beings.
3. (   ) New laws should be passed to limit the amount of pollutants from factories.
4. (   ) There isn't an obvious need to reduce litter and waste in the households.

◆ **Speaking**

Task 1. Talk about the environment problems with your classmates.
Task 2. Two students are in a pair to make a conversation as the following sample.
Sample
David: The air in Beijing is seriously polluted. Look! I can even see the floating dirt overhead.
Li: Yes, air pollution in China is extremely serious, especially in cities with heavy industry.
David: Isn't there any protecting measure adopted by government for the sake of people's health?

Li: There are many. But some depuration devices are not so effective. Some effective devices are so expensive that manufacturers can't even afford.
David: That's it. Then why not consider reducing some heavy industries?
Li: Pretty hard! China is a developing country and needs heavy industries to increase its GDP.
David: How about transferring some plants to suburbs?
Li: It's a good idea! There is a low population density in suburbs so that the harm to people is also slight. However, it brings great inconvenience.

Section II   Passage One

Healthy Lifestyle Helping to Protect the Environment

Over the past few years, most people I've spoken to have become (or already were) environmentally conscious to some degree. What often begins simply as saving money and reducing the amount of electricity you use, which turns out to have quite a positive impact. Here are some lifestyle changes which will help the environment.

Use the car less. This is perhaps the simplest change in this list — reduce the time you spend behind the wheel. In addition to the environmental benefits of doing this, you'll probably find that you become slightly fitter; and have more money in your pocket at the end of the week. In short, there's no downside.

Reduce your intake of red meat. Common sources of red meat such as cows and bulls produce an enormous quantity of climate-changing gases such as methane. I'm certainly not suggesting that you should become vegetarian. I enjoy a good steak as much as any other omnivore, simply that a slight reduction can have a dramatic effect.

Become a "green consumer". When shopping for any sort of product — anything from groceries to a new television, take a moment to weigh up the options. If there are alternatives, consider which product has the lowest impact on the environment.

Become "carbon neutral" using offsets as necessary. This is something that nearly everyone can take advantage of. In effect, you'll be investing in a number of sustainable energy and water schemes.

Share your "green" ideas with others. Over the past century or so, global communications has grown in many, many ways. This has made it possible to share ideas and discoveries at an incredible rate.

Become politically active. By becoming involved in politics at any level with which you feel comfortable. You are able to help guide people to an incredible goal. Rather than sitting back and waiting for someone else to take action, make your own voice heard.

(Words 322)

(Excerpted from http://www.en8848.com.cn/read/bi/2E/109365.html)

New Words（★三级词汇 ◆超纲词汇）

  healthy ['helθɪ]　　*a.* 健康的；强健的

  lifestyle ['laɪfstaɪl]　　*n.* 生活方式

★alternative [ɔːl'tɜːnətɪv]　*a.* 可用以代替其他事物的；另一可选用的；其他的
         n. 可能性中的选择；可能性之一

◆intake ['ɪnteɪk]　*n.* 吸入，纳入（液体、气体等）

  amount [ə'maʊnt]　*n.* (of sth) 总数；总额；总值；数量
        v. (to sth) 总计；共达；等于或相当于某事物

  benefit ['benɪfɪt]　*n.* 利益；实惠；好处

★environmental [ɪn,vaɪərən'mentl]　*a.* 个人环境的；由个人环境产生的；环境的

★environmentally [ɪn,vaɪərən'mentəlɪ]　*ad.* 有关环境方面；环境地

  grocery ['grəʊsərɪ]　*n.* 食品杂货店；食品杂货业

  conscious ['kɒnʃəs]　*a.* 感觉到的；意识到的；清醒的

  carbon ['kɑːbən]　*n.* 碳

  communication [kə,mjuːnɪ'keɪʃn]　*n.* 传递；传播；交流；交换；通信

★global ['gləʊbl]　*a.* 全球性的；全世界的；包括一切的

◆methane ['miːθeɪn]　*n.* 甲烷；沼气

Unit Three　Environment

quantity ['kwɒntətɪ]　*n.* 量；大小；重量；数目；数量
★neutral ['nju:trəl]　*a.* 中立的；不偏不倚的；神经的；神经系统的
◆reduction [rɪ'dʌkʃn]　*n.* 缩减；降低；简化；还原
◆offset ['ɒfset]　*v.* 补偿或抵消某事物
　　　　　　　　　　n. 胶印法

steak [steɪk]　*n.* 肉排；鱼排；（尤指）牛排
◆omnivore ['ɒmnɪvɔ:(r)]　*n.* 杂食动物；杂食者
◆vegetarian [,vedʒɪ'teərɪən]　*n*. 吃素的人
◆sustainable [sə'steɪnəbl]　*a.* 可持续的；可忍受的；可支撑的
★scheme [ski:m]　*n*.计划；方案；阴谋；诡计

Phrases and Expressions

have impact on　对……有影响
in short　简而言之；总之
in effect　实际上，事实上
as much as　差不多
at the end of　在……结尾；在……末端
involve in　参与；涉及；使进入；使卷入

Read and Think

I.　Answer the following questions according to the passage.

1. How many lifestyles are concerned according to the passage?
2. Is the author a vegetarian? Why?
3. Why did the author say "this has made it possible to share ideas and discoveries at an incredible rate"?

Read and Try

II.　Fill in each blank with a right word in its right form using the words in the following box.

lifestyle	amount	intake	global
scheme	grocery	vegetarian	quantity

1. The _____ has been set up to help homeless people.
2. The _____ of gasoline was stopped by a clogged fuel line.

3. All these dishes are suitable for _____.
4. Healthy _____ help us (to) keep in good health.
5. We've always put quality before _____.
6. Our boss has large _____ of mail to answer every day.
7. _____ stores sell many foods that have been processed.
8. The report takes a _____ view of the company's problems.

III. There are eight incomplete sentences below. For each sentence, there are four choices marked A, B, C and D. You should choose the proper one to complete each sentence.

1. Having a _____ and healthy environment is a common goal of humanity.
   A) sustainability   B) sustaining
   C) sustainable   D) sustained

2. The flood resulted in a considerable _____ in production.
   A) reduction   B) reductive
   C) reduce   D) reluctant

3. _____ his poor family condition, the headmaster decided to let him study at school for free.
   A) Consider   B) Considering
   C) Consideration   D) Considered

4. I've had the _____ of a good education.
   A) beneficial   B) beneficiary
   C) benefited   D) benefit

5. It's no use _____ over spilt milk.
   A) weeping   B) crying
   C) laughing   D) smiling

6. His _____ is always consistent with his words.
   A) action   B) active
   C) activity   D) activist

7. He looked tall, handsome and _____.
   A) health   B) healthy
   C) healthful   D) healthily

8. I remember _____ her somewhere before.
   A) seeing   B) to see
   C) to have seen   D) having seen

Unit Three Environment

Read and Translate

IV. Translate the following sentences into English.
1. 他们用钱交换食品，以食品交换钱。总之，他们密切合作。(in short)
2. 在这本书的末尾，情节发生了不寻常的转折。(at the end of)
3. 到杰克生命的最后，实际上他是想重写一切的。(in effect)
4. 父母参与越多，下一代不幸福的几率越大。(involve in)

Reading Skills

Context Clues to Word Meaning

When you come to a new word while reading, you can sometimes figure out what the word means by thinking about the words around it. Words that give you clues about what the new word means are called "context clues" because they give you clues about the meanings of new words. Sometimes the context clues come before the new word and sometimes they come after it. You may find a definition of the new word in the sentence or paragraph. A sentence might have a word that means the opposite of the new word (antonym), and sometimes a synonym, or word that means the same thing as the new word, will give you a clue.

Directions: Read the following paragraphs carefully, and then choose the best answer.

Passage One

Mr. Tritt was a bank clerk. Although he often had the opportunity, he was never able to steal money from a customer. This would have endangered his position at the bank, and he didn't want to <u>jeopardize</u> his future. So he thought he should do something to improve performance and change his fate.

(Words 55)

1. What is the meaning of the underlined word, "jeopardize"?
   A) Prove.   B) Steal.   C) Endanger.   D) Change.

Passage Two

I am not suggesting that we suppress or deny <u>resentment</u>, a feeling of bitterness and anger. But rather, use responsible methods for dealing with these uncomfortable and unpleasant emotions so that we are no longer slaves to the emotional reflexes of our animalistic instincts.

(Words 44)

2. What does the underlined word "resentment" mean?
   A) Animalistic instinct.   B) A feeling of bitterness and anger.

C) Responsible method.　　　　　D) Reflex.

Passage Three

In the past the world seemed to run in an orderly way. Now, however, everything seems to be in a state of <u>turmoil</u>.

(Words 23)

3. What's the meaning of the underlined word?

　A) Orderly　　B) Disordered　　C) Safe.　　D) Stable.

Passage Four

We found that bar at last. I didn't have to ask again, for there it was in big letters over the window—Star Bar. There were some iron tables outside with plastic chairs around them. A few people sat listlessly around, looking at a portable television set that someone had brought out of the bar. They were all in thin summer dresses or short sleeved-shirts; even at that late hour it was <u>stifling</u>. Two thin dogs lay under one of the tables with their tongues out, and some of the women were fanning themselves with magazines.

(Words 96)

4. Which of the following words can replace the underlined word?

　A) Busy.　　B) Early.　　C) Very cold.　　D) Very hot.

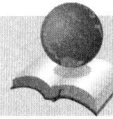

Section II　Passage Two

Protection of the Environment

Man did not have to think about the protection of his environment before. There were few people on the earth, and natural resources seemed to be unlimited. Today things are different. Environmental problems are becoming more and more serious all over the world. With the development of industry and agriculture, cars make great noises and give off poisonous gas. Trees on the hills have been cut down, and waste water is being poured continuously into rivers. Furthermore, wherever we go today, we can find rubbish carelessly disposed. The whole ecological balance of the earth is changing. Massive destruction of environment has brought about negative effects and even poses a great threat to man's existence.

We realize that if too many fish are taken from the sea, there will soon be none left. Yet, with modern fishing methods, more and more fish are caught. We know that if too many trees are cut down, forests will disappear. Yet, we continue to use powerful machines to cut down more and more trees. We see that if rivers are polluted with waste products, we will die. Yet, waste products are still put into rivers. We know that if the population continues to rise at the present rate, in a few years, there won't be enough food. What can we do to solve these problems?

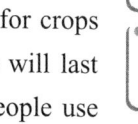

If we eat more vegetables and less meat, there will be more food available. Land for crops feeds five times more people than land where animals are kept. Our natural resources will last longer if we learn to recycle them. The world population will not rise so quickly if people use modern methods of birth control.

Finally, if we educate people to think about the problems we shall have a better and cleaner planet in the future.

(Words 304)

(Excerpted from http://caowu.cn/article/20081221/5662_2.html)

New Words (★三级词汇 ◆超纲词汇)

unlimited [ʌnˈlɪmɪtɪd]   *a.* 尽量多的；任意多的；无限制的
poisonous [ˈpɔɪzənəs]   *a.* 引起中毒的；有毒的
pour [pɔː(r)]   *v.* 使（液体）连续流出；倾倒；倒出
★dispose [dɪˈspəʊz]   *v.* （of）丢掉，消除
◆ecological [ˌiːkəˈlɒdʒɪkl]   *a.* 生态的；生态学的
massive [ˈmæsɪv]   *a.* 巨大的；大而重的；结实的
negative [ˈneɡətɪv]   *a.* 负面的；坏的；否定的
★pose [pəʊz]   *v.* 引起；产生；造成（威胁，问题等）
            n. （为画像，拍照等摆的）姿势
available [əˈveɪləbl]   *a.* 可获得的；可购得的；可找到的
recycle [ˌriːˈsaɪkl]   *v.* 回收利用；再利用

Phrases and Expressions

give off   发出（光等），放出，散发
pour into   川流不息地涌入，源源而来
cut down   砍倒，删减，击倒，杀死
put into   输入，使进入，把……译成，表达

Read and Choose

V. There are five questions or unfinished statements in the following. For each of them there are four choices marked A, B, C and D. Decide the best answer according to Passage Two.

1. Why didn't man have to think about the protection of his environment before?
   A) Because people did not know the environmental problems at that time.
   B) Because people would protect environment at that time.
   C) Because there were few people on the earth and natural resources seemed to be unlimited.
   D) Because people knew how to solve the problem of environment.

2. According to the passage, which of the following statements is not the reason that the environmental problems become more and more serious?
   A) Because of the development of industry and agriculture.
   B) Because people like the present environment.
   C) Because people throw rubbish anywhere they want.
   D) Because the whole ecological balance of the earth is changing.

3. What can we learn from the passage?
   A) Our environmental problems can't be solved in future.
   B) It is necessary to lower the living standards in order to solve the environmental problems.
   C) The whole world has to put a brake on the economy for the environmental problems.
   D) Our environment will become more and more beautiful in future.

4. What can we do to solve the environmental problems according to the passage?
   A) We can learn to recycle natural resources.
   B) We won't eat vegetables and meat any more.
   C) We won't use cars any more.
   D) We should use land for crops only.

5. Which of the following statements is true according to the passage?
   A) Environmental problems are not serious in China.
   B) People can not solve the environmental problems.
   C) Today's environmental problems are the same as before.
   D) Environmental problems are becoming more and more serious all over the world.

VI. In this part, there are five sentences (the first four are taken from the two passages). Below each, there are five Chinese sentences translated, which marked A, B, C, D and E. You should decide which is the best translation.

1. Over the past few years, most people I've spoken to have become (or already were)

Unit Three　Environment

environmentally conscious to some degree. *(Passage One)*

　A. 在过去的几年里，大多数和我说过话的人在某种程度上（或已经）成为环境意识的人。

　B. 在失去的几年中，在某种程度上，大多数我说过话的人变成（或已经）有环保意识。

　C. 在过去的几年里，大部分和我说过话的人都在一定程度上变成（或者本来就是）有环境意识的。

　D. 在过去的几年中，大部分人我说过话的从某种程度上（或已经）是有环境意识的人。

　E. 在失去的几年，我说过话的大多数人（或已经）是有环保意识在某种程度上。

2. Rather than sitting back and waiting for someone else to take action, make your own voice heard. *(Passage One)*

　A. 与其坐在后面等候他人采取行动，不如行动起来让别人看到。

　B. 与其坐等他人行动，倒不如自己行动。

　C. 不是坐在后面等待别人行动起来，而是让人们听到自己的声音。

　D. 不要坐在最后等待他人行动起来，要让人们听到自己的声音。

　E. 与其坐在后面等待别人采取行动，不如让别人看到你的行动。

3. Massive destruction of environment has brought about negative effects and even poses a great threat to man's existence. *(Passage Two)*

　A. 环境的巨大破坏已带来负面影响，甚至严重威胁到大家的生存。

　B. 环境的毁灭已经产生负面作用，甚至严重威胁到大家的生存。

　C. 环境的巨大破坏已经产生负面影响，甚至对大家的生存带来巨大威胁。

　D. 毁灭环境已经产生负面作用，甚至对男人们能否生存提出一个巨大挑战。

　E. 环境的巨大破坏已带来负面影响，甚至对人类生存带来巨大威胁。

4. Land for crops feeds five times more people than land where animals are kept. *(Passage Two)*

　A. 种庄稼用同样大小的土地，会比养殖动物多养活五倍多的人。

　B. 比起养动物，同样大小的土地可以多养活五倍多种庄稼的人。

　C. 同样大小的种庄稼的土地比养殖动物的土地多五倍多。

　D. 同样大小的土地如果种庄稼的话会比养殖动物多养活五倍多的人。

　E. 用同样大小的土地来种庄稼的话，会比保留动物多养活五倍多的人。

5. In choosing a career you should first consider the type of work which will suit your interest.

　A. 在选择一个职业方面，你将首先考虑适合你工作的那种兴趣。

　B. 正在选择一个职业时，你将首先思考满足你利益的那种工作类型。

　C. 在选择职业方面，你应该首先考虑哪种工作适合你的兴趣。

　D. 在选择一个职业方面，你应该首先考虑哪种工作符合你的兴趣。

　E. 在选择职业的时候，你应该首先考虑适合你兴趣的那种工作。

45

Section III Grammar

Gerund（动名词）

动名词也是非限定性动词的一种，由动词原形加尾词-ing 而成，其构成方法与现在分词一样。动名词既有动词性质，又有名词性质。动名词在句中可作主语、表语、宾语、定语、补语等。

动名词分为一般式与完成式：一般式所表示的动作可与谓语动词所表达的动作同时发生；完成式所表达的动作皆发生在谓语动词所表示的动作之前。动名词的被动也有一般式和完成式两种。动名词的否定式由 not 或 never 加动名词构成。

Review and Practice

VII. There are 10 incomplete sentences below. For each one, there are four choices marked A, B, C and D. You should choose the best answer.

1. _____ is a good form of exercises for both young and old.
   A) Walk   B) Walking   C) To walk   D) The walk
2. In the whole interview, he tried to avoid _____ their questions.
   A) to answer   B) answer   C) answering   D) having answered
3. I regret _____ what I said. I shouldn't have said it.
   A) to say   B) to be saying   C) have said   D) saying
4. I understand _____ to discuss the matter.
   A) your not wanting   B) not your wanting
   C) you not to want   D) you want not
5. When you're learning to drive, _____ a good teacher makes a big difference.
   A) have   B) having   C) to have   D) and have
6. He was lucky and narrowly missed _____.
   A) to injure   B) injuring   C) to be injured D) being injured
7. How can you keep the machine _____ when you are away?
   A) run   B) to run   C) running   D) being run
8. It was impolite of him _____ without _____ good-bye.
   A) to leave, saying   B) leaving, to say
   C) to leave, to say   D) leaving, saying

9. We can't imagine _____ in the entrance examination, for she has never been to school.
   A) she succeeding   B) her succeeding
   C) she succeed   D) her to succeed
10. It is no good _____ remember grammatical rules.
    A) trying to   B) to try to   C) try to   D) tried to

VIII. Put the proper forms of the following words in the blanks to complete the sentences.
1. The thief took away the woman's wallet without _____ (see).
2. If I had remembered _____ (lock) the door, the things would not have been stolen.
3. My transistor radio isn't working. It needs _____ (repair).
4. After _____ (get to know) him better, I regretted having judged him unfairly.
5. I'll go with you after I get through with _____ (clean) the house.

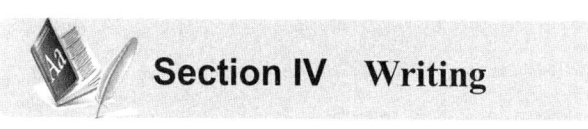

Section IV   Writing

Note for Leaving（请假条）

Note for leaving is one kind of letters. Writing the letter to an employer, teacher or someone else is a very simple and straightforward task. It is necessary to keep the letter short and concise while stating the reason in clear terms. The tone of the letter should be formal and not casual.

Sample

> May. 28
>
> Dear Mr. Wang,
>
> I am writing this letter to ask for your pardon for my absence in your class.
>
> As CET-4 is around the corner, I realized how much I am lagged behind for my preparation schedule. The only choice I have is to borrow some time from my classes for this upcoming exam which is so important for me. I am terribly sorry that I cannot go to your class, and I would be grateful for your understanding.
>
> Thank you for your understanding and I do appreciate it very much. I will make every effort to make up what I may miss from your lesson.
>
> Yours,
> Li Ming

IX. Write a leave letter.

假如你是卢欣。昨天你和同学们去农场帮助农民们摘苹果，不幸从梯子上摔下来伤了腿，但伤得不重。医生建议你在家里好好休息。因此，你向老师 Mr.Smith 请假两天。随信附上医生的证明。

Section V Enjoy Yourselves

A Joke

Einstein climbs to the top of Mt. Sinai to get close enough to talk to God. Looking up, he asks the Lord, "God, what does a million years mean to you?" The Lord replies, "A minute." Einstein asks, "And what does a million dollars mean to you?" The Lord replies, "A penny." Einstein asks, "Can I have a penny?" The Lord replies, "In a minute."

Unit Four Transportation

➢ Warm-up Question

What do you think of the present transportation in the world? Do you think we can live without cars in future?

Section I Listening & Speaking

◆ Listening

Task 1.

Directions: In this section, you will hear 6 short conversations. At the end of each conversation, a question will be asked about what was said. Both the conversation and the question will be spoken twice. After each question there will be a pause. During the pause you must read the four choices marked A), B), C) and D), and decide which is the best answer. Then mark your answer.

Example:

You will hear:

M: Is it possible for you to work late, Miss Green?

W: Work late? I suppose so, if you really think it's necessary.

Q: Where does the conversation most probably take place?

You will read:

A) At the office.

B) In the waiting room.

C) At the airport.

D) In a restaurant.

From the conversation we know that the two were talking about some work they had to finish in the evening. This is most likely to have taken place at the office. Therefore, A) "At the office" is the best answer. You should choose answer A).

Sample Answer

A)   B)   C)   D)

Now let us listen to six short conversations, both the conversation and the question will be spoken twice.

1. A) Bus. B) Plane. C) Taxi. D) Subway.
2. A) 11:20. B) 10:42. C) 11:30. D) 11:12.
3. A) The woman hasn't taken the bus before. B) The man hasn't taken the bus before.
   C) The man has taken the bus before. D) They are friends.
4. A) On the station platform. B) On the train.
   C) On the bus. D) On the plane.
5. A) Take a train south to Liberty Ave. Stop.
   B) Take a train east to Liberty Ave. Stop.
   C) Take a train west to Liberty Ave. Stop.
   D) Take a train north to Liberty Ave. Stop.
6. A) The woman wants to go to Tokyo in September.
   B) The woman wants to book a flight to Tokyo.
   C) The woman wants to book the second flight.
   D) The woman wants to book the flight in September.

Task 2.

Directions: In this section, you will hear a short passage. At the end of the passage, you will hear two questions. Both the passage and the questions will be spoken twice. After you hear a question, you must choose the best answer from the four choices marked A), B), C) and D). Then mark your answer.

1. A) His roommates.
   B) His school fee.
   C) His English ability.
   D) He doesn't have car.
2. A) Driving is a way of life.
   B) There's no public transportation in America.

C) Almost every family needs a car.
D) Many cities have taxis, buses and subways to help commuters get to and from work.

Task 3.

A. Directions: In this section, you will hear a passage three times. Listen carefully during the first reading. Then listen to the passage again. When it is being read the second time, you should fill in the ten blanks numbered from S1) to S10) with the exact words or phrases you have just heard. Finally, when the passage is read for the third time, you should check what you have written.

New Words and Expressions

flexibility [flɛksə'bɪlətɪ] *n.* 灵活
departure [dɪ'pɑːtʃə(r)] *n.* 离开
frequent ['friːkwənt] *a.* 频繁的

    S1) _____ that I had to travel to a place 40 miles away, I would have a choice of several **S2)** _____ transportation. Of course, I could drive my own car, which would give me the greatest flexibility and **S3)** _____. I could **S4)** _____ at any time I liked and would **S5)** _____ drive door-to-door. However, I would have to **S6)** _____ the gas and for a parking place when I arrived. Another option would be to take a bus. This would be cheaper but not as comfortable or **S7)** _____. I could also take a train. This might cost about the same as a bus but **S8)** _____ would probably not be as frequent. However, I could relax on the train and travel in greater **S9)** _____. Finally, I could ride **S10)** _____, but I feel the distance is too great to be comfortable, especially when the weather is bad.

B. Listen to the passage again and then decide whether each of the following statements is true (T) or false (F).

1. (　　) Assuming that I had to travel to a place 40 miles away, I would have a choice of several means of transportation.
2. (　　) I could drive my own car, which would give me the greatest flexibility and independence.
3. (　　) Taking the train costs the same as a bus.
4. (　　) I could ride a motorcycle, but I feel the distance is great to be comfortable, especially if the weather is bad.

◆ **Speaking**

Task 1. Talk about the city transportation with your classmates.

Task 2. Two students are in a pair to make a conversation as the following sample.

Sample

A: Oh, damn! There's another traffic jam on the highway.

B: How can there be a traffic jam on a 16-lane highway every day?

A: There are just too many people, and too many cars.

B: I wonder if there was an accident.

A: No, they just said that too many people were trying to get off at the Capitol exits.

B: Well, let's put on some music. We're going to be stuck in this for a while.

A: All right, what do you want to listen to?

B: How about some Beatles?

A: All right.

Section II   Passage One

The Impact of High-Speed Rail on Civil Aviation

As the Harmony Express pulls into the dirty railway station in China's ancient capital of Xi'an, an army of blue-uniformed attendants busily begin polishing its shining, sleek surface.

This is the face of modern rail in China and the latest addition to a burgeoning high-speed

network that will be the biggest in the world within five years, according to the government's blueprint.

The expansion plans are astonishing: 30,000 km of new track to be laid by the middle of the decade at a cost of as much as RMB 4,000. The results are so impressive that the airline industry is looking on with anxiety.

China's state-controlled carriers are emerging from years of losses and have refocused on the booming domestic travel market, but they are faced with a potentially crippling threat from another arm of the state – the railway sector, led by the Ministry of Railways.

The effect has already been felt on the newly-opened route between Xi'an and Zhengzhou, 505 km away in neighbouring Henan Province. "The airlines have all cancelled their flights to and from Zhengzhou because there aren't enough customers since the high-speed rail line opened," says an official airline ticket vendor in Xi'an airport.

A trip on the Harmony Express (all of the country's new 350 km/h high-speed trains are part of the harmonious network) between Zhengzhou and Xi'an makes it clear why China's airline bosses are so worried.

In the case of Xi'an and Zhengzhou and most other major cities in China, travelers who arrive at the airport must either wait for erratic bus services or stand in line for a taxi to drive more than one hour into town on a newly-built toll road.

In contrast, China's new high-speed trains are clean, fast, smooth and almost always on time. There are no excess baggage fees for heavy luggage. Probably most concerning for airlines is that train tickets are significantly cheaper than airline tickets, especially when the additional costs of taxis and toll road fees are taken into account.

(Words 331)

(Excerpted from http://www.ftchinese.com/story/001032071/ce)

New Words（★三级词汇　◆超纲词汇）

◆impact ['ɪmpækt]　　v.（对某事物）有影响；有作用；冲击；撞击
　　　　　　　　　　n. 巨大影响；强大作用；撞击；冲击力
◆aviation [ˌeɪvɪ'eɪʃn]　n. 航空
★track [træk]　v. 跟随；留下痕迹
　　　　　　　　n. 崎岖不平的小路；火车；轨道；方向
★uniform ['juːnɪfɔːm]　n. 制服；军服
　　　　　　　　　　　a. 一致的；一律的；相同的
　attendant [ə'tendənt]　n. 服务员；侍者；随从；护理员
　　　　　　　　　　　a. 伴随的；随之而来的
◆sleek [sliːk]　v. 使（头发等）发油光；使平整光亮
　　　　　　　a. 光滑的；光亮的；线条流畅的；造型优美的
◆burgeoning ['bɜːdʒənɪŋ]　a. 迅猛发展的；急剧增长的
◆blueprint ['bluːprɪnt]　n. 蓝图；行动方案；模型
★expansion [ɪk'spænʃn]　n. 扩张；扩展；扩大；膨胀
　astonish [ə'stɒnɪʃ]　v. 使十分惊讶；使大为惊奇；使吃惊
★decade ['dekeɪd]　n. 十年；十年期（尤指一个年代）
　anxiety [æŋ'zaɪətɪ]　n. 焦虑；忧虑；害怕；渴望
◆boom [buːm]　n. 激增；繁荣
★domestic [də'mestɪk]　n. 家庭纠纷；家庭矛盾
　　　　　　　　　　　a. 本国的；国内的；家庭的；驯养的
　potential [pə'tenʃl]　n. 可能性；潜在性；潜力；潜质
　　　　　　　　　　　a. 潜在的；可能的
◆cripple ['krɪpl]　v. 使残废；严重毁坏（或损害）
　　　　　　　　n. 残疾人；跛子
★threat [θret]　n. 威胁；恐吓；凶兆；形成威胁的事物
　route [ruːt]　n.（公共汽车和列车等的）常规路线；固定线路；路途；渠道
　cancel ['kænsl]　v. 取消；撤销；终止；注销
　official [ə'fɪʃl]　n. 要员；官员；高级职员
　　　　　　　　　a. 公务的；公职的；正式的；官方的
◆vendor ['vendə(r)]　n. 小贩；摊贩；卖方；供应商
◆erratic [ɪ'rætɪk]　a. 不规则的；不确定的；不稳定的；不可靠的
◆toll [təʊl]　v. 敲（钟）；（尤指）鸣（丧钟）
　　　　　n.（道路、桥梁等的）通行费；毁坏；伤亡人数

★excess [ɪk'ses]   *n.* 超过；过度；过分；放肆行为
                   a. 超额的；额外的；附加的
★significant [sɪg'nɪfɪkənt]   *a.* 有重大意义的；显著的；意味深长的

Phrases and Expressions

pull into   （车、船等）驶入
look on sth./sb. with sth.   （以某种方式）看待
emerge from (sth.)   （从困境或苦难经历中）幸存下来；摆脱出来
makes it clear   弄清楚；讲明
in the case of   至于；就……而言；在……情况下
in contrast   相比之下
take into account   考虑到；顾及

Proper Names

High-Speed Rail   高速铁路
Civil Aviation   民用航空
the Harmony Express   "和谐号"列车
China's state-controlled carriers   中国国有航空公司
the Ministry of Railways   铁道部
excess baggage   （需另收运费的）超重行李

Read and Think

I. **Answer the following questions according to the passage**

1. When will 30,000 km of new track be laid?
2. Why did the airlines cancel their flights to and from Zhengzhou?
3. What is the Harmony Express?

Read and Try

II. **Fill in each blank with a right word in its right form using the words in the following box.**

anxiety	track	domestic	astonish
cancel	potential	decade	additional

1. Prices have risen steadily during the past _____.

2. People all over the world were _____ to have peace.
3. He was determined to _____ down the cause of food spoilage.
4. Another source of considerable urban employment is _____ service.
5. In China, both late marriages and late childbirth are advocated, in _____ to fewer and better births.
6. Her decision to _____ the concert is bound to disappoint her fans.
7. I was _____ at the rapid progress he has made.
8. Education and training are the keys that will unlock our nation's _____.

III. There are eight incomplete sentences below. For each sentence, there are four choices marked A, B, C and D. You should choose the proper one to complete each sentence.

1. It is the first drug that seems to have a very _____ effect on this disease.
   A) significance   B) significantly   C) significancy   D) significant
2. This poses a _____ to agriculture and the food chain, and consequently to human health.
   A) threat   B) threaten   C) threatened   D) threatener
3. A policeman does not wear a _____ when he is off duty.
   A) uniformed   B) uniform   C) uniforms   D) uniformly
4. Whether you drive or take the train, you must be here _____.
   A) in time   B) at times   C) at a time   D) on time
5. Mr. Branson's victory and all the _____ publicity were well deserved.
   A) attend   B) attendant   C) attendee   D) attendance
6. Their economic policies pave the way for industrial _____.
   A) expand   B) expanding   C) expansion   D) expanse
7. He advised his son never to spend in _____ of his income.
   A) excess   B) excessive   C) exceed   D) exceeding
8. Teachers _____ such behavior with disapproval.
   A) look at   B) look on   C) look into   D) look up

Read and Translate

IV. Translate the following sentences into English.
1. 发达国家正极力想摆脱高失业率的困境。(emerge from)
2. 就科学家来说，失败并非羞耻事。(in the case of)
3. 我们务必注意是谁在支持这名候选人。(take into account)
4. 相比之下，权利是指一个人影响决策的能力。(in contrast)

Unit Four Transportation

Reading Skills

Word-part Clues to Word Meaning

If you can't figure out words, one way is to learn word parts: prefixes, roots and suffixes. Prefixes are groups of letters with meanings that appear in front of a word; suffixes appear at the end of a word. The root or stem is the basic part of a word. Learning meanings of word parts can save your time and increase your word power.

Directions: Read the following paragraphs carefully, and then figure out the underlined words.

Passage One

The reasons for a visit to a lighthouse are not all so backward-looking in time. It is true that lighthouses were built in <u>out-of-the-way</u> places. But on a pleasant sunny summer day, this very isolation has a natural beauty that many people will love to experience.

(Words 46)

1. The underlined "out-of-the-way" means _____.

Passage Two

From Eliot's viewpoint, the other key to controlling stress is to "realize that there are other <u>troublesome</u> parts of your life over which you can have little or no control—like the economy and politicians." You have to realize that sometimes with things like traffic jams, deadlines and unpleasant bosses, "You can't fight. You can't flee. You have to learn how to flow."

(Words 63)

2. The underlined word "troublesome" means _____.

Passage Three

"That's very common in professional women. They feel they have to be all things to all people and do it all perfectly. They think, 'I should, I must, I have to.' Good enough is never good enough. <u>Perfectionists</u> cannot delegate. They get angry that they have to carry it all, and they blow their tops. Then they feel guilty and they start the whole cycle over again."

(Words 67)

3. The underlined word "Perfectionists" means _____.

Passage Four

The main predictors of <u>destructive</u> levels of stress are the FUD factors—fear, uncertainty and doubt—together with perceived lack of control, he says. For many people, the root of their stress is anger, and the trick is to find out where the anger is coming from. "Does the anger come from a feeling that everything must be perfect?" Eliot asks.

(Words 61)

57

4. The underlined word "destructive" means _____.

Section II Passage Two

Children Say They Prefer Daddy to Drive

Women drivers have long faced slurs from men over their prowess behind the wheel. Now it seems even their children are critics.

Research among youngsters has found 47 percent feel unsafe being driven by their mothers, compared with 39 percent who feel unsafe with their fathers.

Despite parents insisting they drive more cautiously when transporting their children, the survey found large numbers do not feel secure with either parent.

Nearly 5 percent confessed to being scared if they have to climb into a car with their parents.

The survey of 500 children aged ten to sixteen across Britain found 9 percent had been in an accident with their mothers driving and 8 percent with their fathers'.

However, the flaws in mothers' driving spotted by young backseat drivers were different to those committed by fathers.

The study found the most common complaint was 24 percent saying their mother was bad at parking, followed by 21 percent saying their father drove too fast.

Women are better at finding the car keys than their scatty spouses.

Fathers are more likely to drink and drive than mothers, with 8 percent of children commenting on their fathers getting behind the wheel after consuming alcohol compared with 2 percent saying the same about their mothers.

Six percent complained their mothers drove too fast.

Jennifer Culley, from Privilege Insurance, which carried out the study, said: "With almost one in 20 children actually scared by their parents' driving, 'grown-ups' need to drive even more carefully and follow the rules of the road."

"Driving safely will help to put children's minds at ease, as well as demonstrate how they should drive in the future."

Robin Cummins, road safety consultant for the British School of Motoring, said that children can subconsciously copy their parents' bad driving habits when they become adults.

(Words 302)

(Excerpted from <http://www.chinadaily.com.cn/language_tips/ 2007-05/25/content_880253.htm>)

New Words（★三级词汇　◆超纲词汇）

◆slur [slɜ:(r)]　　*v.* 诽谤；诋毁；污辱；含糊不清地说话
　　　　　　　　　n. 诽谤；诋毁；污辱
◆prowess ['praʊəs]　　*n.* 非凡的技能；高超的技艺；造诣
★critic ['krɪtɪk]　　*n.* 批评家；评论家；评论员；挑剔的人
　youngster ['jʌŋstə(r)]　　*n.* 年轻人；少年；儿童
　cautious ['kɔ:ʃəs]　　*a.* 小心的；谨慎的
★confess [kən'fes]　　*v.* 供认；坦白；承认；忏悔
　scare [skeə(r)]　　*v.* 惊吓；使害怕；使恐惧
　　　　　　　　　n. 恐慌；恐惧；惊吓；惊恐
◆flaw [flɔ:]　　*n.* 错误；缺点；裂痕；瑕疵
★commit [kə'mɪt]　　*v.* 做出（错或非法的事）；犯（罪或错等）
★complaint [kəm'pleɪnt]　　*n.* 抱怨；埋怨；投诉；控告
◆scatty ['skætɪ]　　*a.* 健忘的；傻乎乎的
　consume [kən'sju:m]　　*v.* 消耗；耗费；吃；烧毁
　grown-up [ɡrəʊn-ʌp]　　*n.* 大人；成人
　　　　　　　　　a. 成熟的；成年的；长大的
　demonstrate ['demənstreɪt]　　*v.* 证明；证实；表达；示范
★consultant [kən'sʌltənt]　　*n.* 顾问；高级顾问医师；会诊医师

◆ subconscious [ˌsʌbˈkɒnʃəs]   *a.* 下意识的；潜意识的

Phrases and Expressions

behind the wheel 在驾驶；在操舵；控制；掌管
comment on 评论；注释
carry out 执行；实现；完成
at ease 舒适；自在；无拘无束

Read and Choose

V. There are five questions or unfinished statements in the following. For each of them there are four choices marked A, B, C and D. Decide the best answer according to Passage Two.

1. Which of the following statements is true according to the passage?
   A) 47 percent youngsters felt unsafe being driven by their fathers.
   B) 24 percent youngsters said their fathers were bad at parking.
   C) 8 percent children had been in an accident with their mother driving.
   D) Nearly 5 percent children actually scared by their parents' driving.

2. How old are the children who couldn't take part in the survey?
   A) 12.   B) 14.   C) 15.   D) 17.

3. In what aspects are women better than men according to the author?
   A) Parking.   B) Driving.
   C) Finding the car keys.   D) Following the rules of the road.

4. According to the survey, how many children commented on their mothers getting behind the wheel after consuming alcohol?
   A) 40.   B) 10.   C) 120.   D) 105.

5. What does the word "consultant" in the last paragraph probably mean?
   A) A person who gives expert advice to a person or organization.
   B) A company that gives expert advice on a particular subject.
   C) An experienced doctor who specializes in one area of medicine.
   D) A lawyer who pleads cases in court.

VI. In this part, there are five sentences (the first four are taken from the two passages). Below each, there are five Chinese sentences translated, which marked A, B, C, D and E. You should decide which is the best translation.

Unit Four　Transportation

1. A trip on the Harmony Express between Zhengzhou and Xi'an makes it clear why China's airline bosses are so worried. (***Passage One***)

    A) 在和谐号列车上旅游郑州和西安，能明确为什么中国航空公司的老板会那么担忧。

    B) 坐一次郑州和西安之间的和谐号列车，就清楚为什么中国航空公司的头头们会那么焦虑了。

    C) 在和谐号列车上游览一次郑州和西安，就能知道为什么中国航空公司的老板会那么担忧。

    D) 坐过郑州到西安的和谐号列车一次后，就能明白中国航空公司的头头们为什么如此焦虑了。

    E) 只需坐一次郑州至西安的和谐号列车，就能明白中国各航空公司的头头们为何如此焦虑不安了。

2. In contrast, China's new high-speed trains are clean, fast, smooth and almost always on time. (***Passage One***)

    A) 与之相比，中国新到的高速列车是干净、迅速、流畅的，而且总是准时的。

    B) 相比之下，中国崭新的高铁列车干净、快速、平稳，几乎从不晚点。

    C) 与之相比，中国现代的高速列车是整洁、快捷、流畅的，而且一直很及时。

    D) 相比之下，中国新的高速列车是干净、快速、平稳的，而且总是准时的。

    E) 相比之下，中国崭新的高铁列车干净、快速、平稳，而且差不多一直准点。

3. Women drivers have long faced slurs from men over their prowess behind the wheel. (***Passage Two***)

    A) 女性司机长期面临着男性对于她们在车辆后面的技术的诋毁。

    B) 女性司机长期面临着男性对于她们驾车技术的轻视。

    C) 女司机们把控方向盘的能力总是受到男同胞们的鄙视。

    D) 女司机们总是受到男同胞们对于她们开车技术的轻视。

    E) 女司机们总是受到男同胞们对于她们掌控方向盘的能力的鄙视。

4. Fathers are more likely to drink and drive than mothers. (***Passage Two***)

    A) 爸爸们比起妈妈们更有可能酒后开车。

    B) 爸爸们喝酒开车的几率比妈妈大。

    C) 妈妈们比起爸爸们更有可能酒后开车。

    D) 爸爸们酒后开车的几率比妈妈大。

    E) 妈妈们比起爸爸更喜欢喝酒和开车。

5. It's rare to find an American teenager without a driver's license.

    A) 找到一个没有驾照的美国青年是很容易的。

    B) 在美国要找到一个没有驾照的青少年是很不容易的。

C) 找到一个有驾照的美国青年是很不容易的。

D) 在美国要找到一个没有驾照的青少年是很容易的。

E) 很少能找到一个没有驾照的美国青年。

Section III Grammar

Noun Clauses（名词性从句）

英语中的从句分为主语从句、表语从句、宾语从句、同位语从句、定语从句和状语从句六类。由于主语从句、表语从句、宾语从句和同位语从句在句子中的功能相当于名词，故这四种从句又统称为名词性从句。名词性从句所用关联词大抵相同，而且其前面一般不用逗号，常见的有关系代词 what, whatever, who, whoever, whom, whomever, whose, which, whichever, 关系副词 when, where, how, why, whenever, wherever, however, 从属连词 that, whether, if, as if, as though.

Review and Practice

VII. There are 10 incomplete sentences below. For each one, there are four choices marked A, B, C and D. You should choose the best answer.

1. _____ David says sounds right to Helen. That's why she has made up her mind to leave him _____ happens.

   A) Whatever; whatever   B) No matter what; whatever
   C) No matter what; no matter what   D) Whatever; however

2. That is _____ I was born and grew up.

   A) there   B) in which
   C) where   D) the place

3. _____ she was invited to the ball made her very happy.

   A) What   B) That
   C) When   D) Because

4. _____ we are doing has never been done before.

   A) That   B) What
   C) Which   D) Whether

5. —Have you found your book yet?

Unit Four   Transportation

—No, I'm not sure _____ I could have left it.
A) whether   B) where
C) when   D) why

6. The doctor couldn't answer the question _____ the patient could survive that night.
A) if   B) that
C) whether   D) what

7. I firmly believe _____ he said at the meeting was right.
A) that   B) which
C) that what   D) what that

8. —What were you trying to prove to the police?
   —_____ I was last night.
A) That   B) When
C) Where   D) What

9. I think, though I could be mistaken, _____ he liked me.
A) who   B) which
C) that   D) what

10. At the meeting, we discussed _____ we should employ more workers.
A) if   B) whether
C) that   D) /

VIII. Correct the errors in the following sentences.

1. The driver could not control his car was obvious.
2. If he left or not is unknown.
3. He said that he had eaten nothing but he wasn't hungry.
4. Tom thought how beautiful girl Mary was.
5. I think he won't win the game, will he?

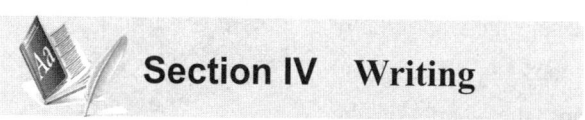

Section IV Writing

Poster（海报）

A poster is any piece of printed paper designed to be attached to a wall or vertical surface. Posters are designed to be both eye-catching and convey information. They are a frequent tool of advertisers (particularly of events, musicians and films), propagandists, protestors and other groups trying to communicate a message.

Sample

POSTER

Basketball Match

Sichuan Team vs. Shanghai Team

Time: 3:00 p. m., Sep. 6th

Place: The City Stadium

Please contact the Physical Culture Group.

Tickets are limited. Fans should be quick.

The Physical Culture Group

September 3rd, 2014

IX. Write an English poster.

2015 年 5 月 15 日晚 7 点，在第一教学楼 B109 教室有一场关于美国南北战争的讲座，由外语系组织发起。主讲人是最近来我校访问的美国南加利福尼亚大学的琼斯教授。欢迎广大师生参加。

Section V   Enjoy Yourselves

The Origin of Hot Dogs

The origin of hot dogs actually dates back to over five hundred years in the past. It is believed that hot dogs were made in Germany first and it was definitely not named hot dog back then! The sausage was actually named by a butcher in Frankfurt, Germany as "dachshund sausage", after his pet dachshund. Perhaps the shape of the dachshund, which is a small dog with a long and slender body,  caused the butcher to see the resemblance between his sausages and his dog. Thus the name "dachshund sausage" came to existence. How the name changed from dachshund sausage to hotdog is another, highly controversial story.

Douglas B. Smith mentioned in his book that the credit of the name should go to the cartoonist T.A. Dorgan of the "New York Journal". According to the story that Smith wrote in his book "Ever Wonder Why", T.A. Dorgan was enjoying a baseball match back in 1901, when he heard vendors yelling to sell their "hot dachshund sausages". The situation drew the attention of Dorgan and being a cartoonist by profession, he made a cartoon sketch of the whole situation but being unsure about the actual spelling of the term "dachshund", he gave it the name of "hot dog". This is the most popular theory about the origin of the name hot dog.

It is to be noted that the above theory regarding the origin of the hot dog is not proven to be the absolute. Also, the various details may vary widely with each website or book that you would come across. For example, the year is found to be 1906 in place of 1901 in some cases, while some claim that it was not a baseball match but a polo game. Others claim that it was neither a baseball match, nor was it a polo game; rather it was a six-day bicycle race. Which of these facts are true or if all of them are false, is something that is hard to tell accurately now, but what it does suggest is that the story is doubtful. There are other theories also, which stem from the fact that the term hot dog was in use even before TAD or Dorgan used it to depict his cartoon.

Unit Five   Science & Technology

➢ Warm-up Question

In what ways has science changed our life?

Section I   Listening & Speaking

◆ Listening

Task 1.

Directions: In this section, you will hear 6 short conversations. At the end of each conversation, a question will be asked about what was said. Both the conversation and the question will be spoken twice. After each question there will be a pause. During the pause you must read the four choices marked A), B), C) and D), and decide which is the best answer. Then mark your answer.

Example:
You will hear:
M: Is it possible for you to work late, Miss Green?
W: Work late? I suppose so, if you really think it's necessary.
Q: Where does the conversation most probably take place?

You will read:
A) At the office.
B) In the waiting room.
C) At the airport.
D) In a restaurant.

From the conversation we know that the two were talking about some work they had to finish in the evening. This is most likely to have taken place at the office. Therefore, A) "At the office" is the best answer. You should choose answer A).

Sample Answer

~~A)~~   B)   C)   D)

New Words and Expressions

★function ['fʌŋkʃn]   *n.* 作用；功能
                      v. 起作用

Now let us listen to 6 short conversations, both the conversation and the question will be spoken twice.

1. A) A new mobile phone.   B) A video recording.
   C) A music player.   D) A motor cycle.
2. A) Mary doesn't think the dish is delicious.
   B) Mary doesn't like the dish.
   C) The dish was cooked by a famous cook.
   D) The dish was cooked by a robot.
3. A) In the library.   B) In the laboratory.
   C) In the cinema.   D) In the supermarket.
4. A) At home.   B) In the park.
   C) In the net bar.   D) On the campus.
5. A) There is nothing wrong with the man's computer.
   B) There are many problems with the man's computer.
   C) The man's computer is a new one.
   D) The woman cannot repair the computer.
6. A) 4,500.   B) 4,100.
   C) 400.   D) 500.

Task 2.

Directions: In this section, you will hear a short passage. At the end of the passage, you will hear two questions. Both the passage and the questions will be spoken twice. After you hear one question, you must choose the best answer from the four choices marked A), B), C) and D). Then mark your answer.

New Words and Expressions

★critical ['krɪtɪkl]   *a.* 关键的；批判性的

★stroke [strəʊk]   *n.* 笔画

　　　　　　　　　v. 轻抚

◆activate ['æktɪveɪt]   *v.* 使活动；激活

◆boost [buːst]   *v.* 使增长；增强；提高

◆fine-motor   小肌肉群运动

1. A) Handwriting has become a dying art.
   B) Now kids start using keyboards as soon as they begin school.
   C) Writing by hand is different from typing.
   D) A study found that children who practiced printing by hand had less active brains than kids who simply looked at letters.

2. A) To learn letters and shapes.
   B) To improve their composition of ideas.
   C) To boost fine-motor skills development.
   D) All of the above.

Task 3.

A. Directions: In this section, you will hear a passage three times. Listen carefully during the first reading. Then listen to the passage again. When it is being read the second time, you should fill in the ten blanks numbered from S1) to S10) with the exact words or phrases you have just heard. Finally, when the passage is read for the third time, you should check what you have written.

New Words and Expressions

★gravity ['grævətɪ]   *n.* 重力；地球引力

◆flush [flʌʃ]   *v.* 冲洗；脸红

★vacuum ['vækjuəm]   *n.* 真空

　suck [sʌk]   *v.* 吮；吸

◆thigh [θaɪ]   *n.* 大腿

◆NASA ['næsə]   （美国）国家航空和航天局

　　Going to the toilet is easy down here on Earth, because **S1)** _____ pulls your solid and liquid wastes down, away from you. But in the gravity-free **S2)** _____ of space, waste tends to just **S3)** _____. Since the early days of the space flight, NASA has learned a lot about what to do with human waste while their **S4)** _____ are away from Mother Earth. Now, space toilets look similar to the Western **S5)** _____ toilets that people use on Earth. However, **S6)** _____ flushing, they work like a **S7)** _____ cleaner sucking away the astronaut's waste. When **S8)** _____ calls, astronauts fasten their bodies to the toilet so that they won't float away. They are held on by a bar **S9)** _____ their thighs. There are different ways of treating solid and liquid waste. All solid waste is brought back to Earth for **S10)** _____, while liquid waste is thrown out into space from time to time.

B. Listen to the passage again and then decide whether each of the following statements is true (T) or false (F).

1. (   ) Going to the toilet is difficult down here on Earth.
2. (   ) NASA has learned little about what to do with human waste while their astronauts are away from Mother Earth.
3. (   ) Now, space toilets look similar to the Western style toilets that people use on Earth.
4. (   ) All liquid waste is brought back to Earth for treatment, while solid waste is thrown out into space from time to time.

◆ **Speaking**

Task 1. Talk about the advantages and disadvantages of science and technology with your classmates.

Task 2. Two students are in pair to make a conversation as the following sample.

Sample

Linda: Look, somebody is flying a kite. How beautiful!
Jack: That dragonfly-shaped kite flies quite high.
Linda: That little string can take the kite up to the sky; that's really something!
Jack: Flying kites is popular in many countries. Are they from China?
Linda: Yes, according to tradition the kite was invented by Lu Ban two thousand years ago.
Jack: Is it complicated to make a kite?
Linda: No, we can make one ourselves. But it won't be beautiful as the ones they sell.

Section II Passage One

Wash. U. Scientists Discover Mind-Reading

It sounds like something from a science-fiction novel: communicating with another person not by speaking or gesticulating, but simply by thinking.

Mental telepathy? Mumbo-jumbo, right?

No. According to scientists at the Washington University School of Medicine, this form of communication has been occurring for a while in their labs, marking the first occasions in which a person's thoughts have been channelled across a computer screen.

"We are truly starting to read the language of thought," author Eric C. Leuthardt said in a university news release. "This is one of the earliest examples, to a very, very small extent, of what is called 'reading minds'—detecting what people are saying to themselves in their internal dialogue."

The secret lies in a small surgical implant—embedded in a patient's brain—which is programmed to identify certain brainwave patterns that get activated when the patient thinks about a specific sound.

There are huge applications for people who've suffered from brain damage.

Here's the method: Test subjects (in this case, epilepsy patients) were outfitted with brain-computer interfaces, which were implanted in the regions of the brain controlling speech. Patients then were instructed to think about one of four particular sounds ("oo", "ee", "ay" or "a"). The act of thinking about those sounds created brainwave patterns that the interfaces identified and transmitted to a computer screen. By the end of the experiment, patients could control the movement of a cursor on a computer monitor simply by thinking of a particular sound.

The research was published this week in *The Journal of Neural Engineering.*

So, it's pretty spooky to think about how far this research can go—and what could happen if the technology were to be adopted for non-therapeutic purposes. It's conceivable that the day will come when we can all get our heads implanted and have computer-assisted conversations with family members scattered across the country—without even opening our mouths or striking a keypad.

The only thing we need to do is to think.

(Words 342)

(Excerpted from <http://blogs.riverfronttimes.com/dailyrft/2011/04/brain_computer_communication_washington_university.php>   By John H. Tucker)

New Words（★三级词汇 ◆超纲词汇）

◆gesticulate [dʒeˈstɪkjuleɪt]   *v.* 做手势；用手势表达；用动作示意

◆telepathy [təˈlepəθɪ]   *n.* 传心术；通灵术；心灵感应

◆mumbo-jumbo [ˌmʌmbəʊ-ˈdʒʌmbəʊ]   *n.* 胡言乱语；繁文缛节

　release [rɪˈliːs]   *n.* 释放；发布；发行

　detect [dɪˈtekt]   *v.* 发现；查明；探测

★surgical [ˈsɜːdʒɪkl]   *a.* 外科的；外科手术的

◆implant [ˈɪmplɑːnt]   *n.*（植入人体中的）植入物

　　　　[ɪmˈplɑːnt]   *v.* 灌输；将……植入

◆embed [ɪmˈbed]   *v.* 把……牢牢地嵌入（或插入、埋入）

　brainwave [ˈbreɪnweɪv]   *n.* 灵感；妙计；脑电波

　application [ˌæplɪˈkeɪʃn]   *n.* 申请；请求；应用；运用

◆epilepsy [ˈepɪlepsɪ]   *n.* 癫痫

◆outfit [ˈaʊtfɪt]   *n.* 全套服装；团队

　　　　　　v. 装备；配置设备

◆interface [ˈɪntəfeɪs]   *n.*（人机）界面；接口

　　　　　　v. 接合；连接

　region [ˈriːdʒən]   *n.* 地区；区域；行政区

★cursor [ˈkɜːsə(r)]   *n.*（计算机荧光屏上的）光标；游标

◆spooky [ˈspuːkɪ]   *a.* 怪异吓人的

★adopt [əˈdɒpt]   *v.* 收养；采用；正式通过；选定

◆therapeutic [ˌθerə'pjuːtɪk]   *a.* 治疗的；医疗的；有助于放松精神的
◆conceivable [kən'siːvəbl]   *a.* 可想象的；可信的
★scattered ['skætəd]   *a.* 分散的；零散的；疏落的
◆keypad ['kiːpæd]   *n.* 小键盘；按键

Phrases and Expressions

science-fiction novel 科幻小说
to...extent 到……程度；在……程度上

Proper Names

Washington University 华盛顿大学

Read and Think

I. Answer the following questions according to the passage.

1. What special form of communication has been occurring for a while in their labs according to the scientists at Washington University School of Medicine?
2. What is called "reading minds" according to Paragraph 4?
3. How could patients control the movement of a cursor on a computer monitor?

Read and Try

II. Fill in each blank with a right word in its right form using the words in the following box.

| region | channel | application | suffer |
| detect | communication | release | mental |

1. Radar is used to _____ objects in the air or at sea.
2. The warm _____ is crowded with birds.
3. Speech is the fastest method of _____ between people.
4. The film is scheduled for _____ next month.
5. The new invention would have a wide range of _____ in industry.
6. The doctor is trying to solve his _____ problem.
7. Many companies are _____ from a shortage of skilled staff.
8. Money for the project will be _____ through local government.

III. There are eight incomplete sentences below. For each sentence, there are four choices marked A, B, C and D. You should choose the proper one to complete each sentence.

1. The old couple decided to _____ a boy and a girl though they had had three of their own.
   A) adapt   B) bring
   C) receive   D) adopt

2. The thieves _____ the papers all over the room as they were searching for the money.
   A) spread   B) swelled
   C) scattered   D) divided

3. It is useful to be able to predict the extent _____ which a price change will affect supply and demand.
   A) from   B) with
   C) to   D) for

4. The factory was built in a secret place, around _____ high mountains.
   A) it was   B) which were
   C) them were   D) which was

5. _____ is mentioned above that the number of the students in senior school is increasing.
   A) Which   B) As
   C) That   D) It

6. They put forward a lot of plans at the meeting, but none of _____ were carried out in their work.
   A) which   B) them
   C) what   D) that

7. The time when a solar eclipse(日食) will _____ can be calculated.
   A) happen   B) take place
   C) occur   D) be occurred

8. He always has a lot of _____ ideas in his mind, and sometimes we do not even know what he is thinking about.
   A) novel   B) spoil
   C) acceptable   D) additional

Read and Translate

IV. Translate the following sentences into English.
1. 这听起来像个久远的故事。(sound like)
2. 可以相信他到什么程度？ (to what extent)

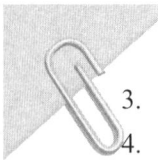

3. 所有经济部门都遭受到这次汇率下跌带来的损失。(suffer from)
4. 你能在本周末之前背熟这部分吗？(by the end of)

Reading Skills

Signal Words

While reading, some words are so important that they can help you understand the passage. They function like traffic lights or road signs to guide the reader smoothly along the path of thought set down by the writer, so we call them signal words. It's necessary to understand what signal words are and how they function.

They can be found anywhere in a paragraph or can be used to form a closer tie between paragraphs. And, they can be classified according to their functions. They may introduce examples, or show a change of thought, or express causes/effects, or lead to additional information, or indicate sequence of events/ideas, or draw a conclusion and so on.

Directions: Read the following paragraphs carefully, and then find out the signal words in each of the following passages.

Passage One

Children's education is changing very fast today. In the past, teachers made children sit quietly for hours. They made them remember all kinds of things. The children had to go on reading things again and again until they knew them "by heart". Today, many teachers wonder if it is possible to make children learn all the things. They say you can only help them learn. They say you must let children learn and discover things by themselves.

(Words 74)

1. _____

Passage Two

As a matter of fact, music is an expression of the people. As you research, you will find music of people a love of nature and at work or at party. You will find it can express love of the country, love of nature and love of home. Music is also an expression of the computer. The composer expresses his own music ideas. He studies the materials of music and discovers the use of them. He looks for new kinds of musical expressions.

(Words 64)

2. _____

Passage Three

For instance, when in a new situation, an intelligent person thinks about the situation, not about himself or what might happen to him. He tries to find out all he can, and then he acts immediately and tries to do something about it. He probably isn't sure how it will all work out, but just tries to learn from his mistakes. An intelligent person, even if he is very young, has a special outlook on life, a special feeling about life, and knows how he fits into it.

(Words 64)

3. _____

Passage Four

By the year 2400, the air is too polluted for humans to breath. So we have to leave the earth. But only the rich are able to leave. Where will we go? No where. You see scientists do not find another safe planet, so now we must travel around the universe in our spaceships. We are still looking for a place to call our home.

(Words 73)

4. _____

Section II Passage Two

Exploring 3D Technology: From Cinema to Home

As more "3D" films hit theaters, the next phase of advanced techniques will be geared towards home devices like televisions and personal computers. By the middle of this year, it will be possible to tap into this amazing technology.

With the popularity of Avatar, audience wearing 3D glasses has become an increasingly common sight in cinemas all over the world. With a special pair of 3D glasses, moviegoers will experience more thrills than they ever did before. Moviegoer said, "It almost makes it more of an interactive process when you are being entertained by the film. It captivates you more. It brings you more into the story. There is more entertainment value in a 3D film because of the level of stimulation that is not provided by standard film."

But that thrill is about to come from home.

XpanD, a Los Angeles based company, is currently the only creator of active 3D glasses for theaters in the US. This year, it is about to launch state-of-the-art glasses for home use. That means with a TV, or computer installed with the right program, people can enjoy a 3D ride without leaving their homes.

Maria Costiera, XpanD CEO, said, "I'm talking something that you're going to watch TV with, that the kids are going to play computer games with and that you will watch your football game with. You're going to go into the cinema with your own pair."

The business could be a promising venture. Some big companies are already showing interest in producing home viewing devices with 3D features built in.

Since the first motion picture in 1895, the movie industry has undergone tremendous generational change, and so have our watching habits. Now, with the advent of this latest 3D technology, perhaps we will leap into the next phase of evolutionary viewing.

(Words 302)

(Excerpted from <http://english.cctv.com/program/worldwidewatch/
20100106/103757.shtml> Editor: Zheng Limin）

New Words（★三级词汇 ◆超纲词汇）

★phase [feɪz]   *n.* 阶段；时期
      v. 分阶段进行；逐步做
★technique [tek'ni:k]   *n.* 技巧；工艺；技术
◆gear [gɪə(r)]   *n.* 排挡；齿轮
     v. 使与……相适应
popularity [ˌpɒpju'lærəti]   *n.* 受欢迎；普及；流行
◆moviegoer ['mu:vɪɡəʊə(r)]   *n.* （经常）上电影院的人；爱看电影者
◆thrill [θrɪl]   *n.* 兴奋感；激动
    v. 使非常兴奋；使非常激动
◆interactive [ˌɪntər'æktɪv]   *a.* 合作的；相互影响的；互动的
◆captivate ['kæptɪveɪt]   *v.* 迷住；使着迷
★stimulation [ˌstɪmju'leɪʃn]   *n.* 刺激
 promising ['prɒmɪsɪŋ]   *a.* 有希望的；有前途的；有出息的
★motion ['məʊʃn]   *n.* 运动；动作
 undergo [ˌʌndə'ɡəʊ]   *v.* 经历；经受
★evolutionary [ˌi:və'lu:ʃənrɪ]   *a.* 进化的；演变的

Phrases and Expressions

◆gear sth. towards/to sth.   使与……相适应；使适合于

Unit Five   Science & Technology

◆tap into 利用，开发，发掘
state-of-the-art 最先进的
motion picture 电影

Read and Choose

V. There are five questions or unfinished statements in the following. For each of them there are four choices marked A, B, C and D. Decide the best answer according to Passage Two.

1. From the first paragraph, we can infer that _____.
   A) theaters have met a big failure because of 3D
   B) 3D's entering our home has been a clear trend
   C) 3D technology will be used in almost anything
   D) people have known how to wear 3D glasses

2. The second paragraph mainly tells us about _____.
   A) differences between 3D and standard films
   B) the popularity of the movie Avatar
   C) the advantages of 3D glasses
   D) the disadvantages of 3D glasses

3. This year, XpanD is about to launch state-of-the-art glasses for home use. What does that mean?
   A) Audience wearing 3D glasses has become an increasingly common sight in cinemas all over the world.
   B) There is more entertainment value in a 3D film because of the level of stimulation that is not provided by standard film.
   C) With a TV, or computer installed with the right program, people can enjoy a 3D ride without leaving their homes.
   D) You're going into the cinema with your own partner.

4. What are 3D glasses according to Maria Costiera?
   A) They are something that you're going to watch TV with.
   B) They are something that the kids are going to play computer games with.
   C) They are something that you will watch your football game with.
   D) All of the above.

5. The word "venture" in the sixth paragraph means _____.
   A) adventure   B) capital

C) schedule   D) project

VI. In this part, there are five sentences (the first four are taken from the two passages). Below each, there are five Chinese sentences translated, which marked A, B, C, D and E. You should decide which is the best translation.

1. It sounds like something from a science-fiction novel: communicating with another person not by speaking or gesticulating, but simply by thinking. *(Passage One)*

    A) 这听起来就像是演科幻小说一样：同其他人之间的交流不是说话或表情，而只是简单地通过思考就能达到目的。

    B) 这听起来就像是科幻小说里的情节：人们之间交流不用说话或用肢体语言，而只是简单通过思考就能达到目的。

    C) 在科幻小说里，人们之间的感情交流是不需要语言和形体的，只要人们可以独立思考问题就能做到。

    D) 这听起来像从科幻小说出来的东西：与他人的沟通不可以说话或打手势，而是要在思考之后。

    E) 这听起来就像是科幻小说里的情节：人们之间交流不用说话或指手划脚，而只是通过简单的思考就能达到目的。

2. It's pretty spooky to think about how far this research can go—and what could happen if the technology were to be adopted for non-therapeutic purposes. *(Passage One)*

    A) 想想这项研究的未来不禁让人毛骨悚然。如果这种技术不是用在治病救人上，那又会产生怎样的后果呢？

    B) 想到这项研究的未来人们不禁毛骨悚然。如果这项技术被非医疗机构采用，那又会产生怎样的后果呢？

    C) 想想这项研究的未来不禁让人觉得诡异。如果这种技术不是用来治病救人，那又会产生什么样的后果呢？

    D) 想到这项研究可以有多大进展，人们不禁觉得好奇。如果这种技术采用非医疗手段，那又该怎么办呢？

    E) 说到这项研究的未来人们不禁有些担心。如果发明这种技术的目的是非医疗的，那又会出什么事呢？

3. As more "3D" films hit theaters, the next phase of advanced techniques will be geared towards home devices like televisions and personal computers. *(Passage Two)*

    A) 因为越来越多 3D 电影的上映，这项先进技术下一阶段将面向家庭，着眼于像电视机和个人电脑这样的家庭设备。

    B) 很多 3D 电影突然袭击了很多剧院，所以下一阶段的任务是先进的技术将用在个人电脑里代替家庭设备中的电视机。

C) 随着越来越多 3D 电影的上映，这项先进技术下一阶段将面向家庭，着眼于像电视机和个人电脑这样的家庭设备。

D) 因为很多 3D 电影上映，先进的技术在下一阶段将应用于电视机和个人电脑这样的家庭设备。

E) 当很多 3D 电影的上映时，先进的技术得以采用，下一阶段将适用于像电视机和个人电脑这样的家庭设备。

4. That means with a TV, or computer installed with the right program, people can enjoy a 3D ride without leaving their homes. *(Passage Two)*

A) 它的意思是电视机安装在右侧的计算机的程序里，人们可以无需离开自己的家园也能骑车享受 3D 电视。

B) 这就意味着只要在电脑或电视机上装入正确的程序，人们就算足不出户也能享受一次 3D 之旅。

C) 这意味着，或者有了正确的程序安装的计算机，人们可以无需离开自己的家园也能骑车享受 3D 电视。

D) 这就意味着只要在电脑或电视机上装入正确的程序，人们不离开家也能通过 3D 享受一次旅行。

E) 这就是说只要电脑电视机的程序安装都正确的话，人们就是不离开家也能享受一次 3D 之旅。

5. People now have more leisure time, which is the reason why the demand for services has increased so rapidly.

A) 如今人们有更多的时间去娱乐，从而影响了劳务资源的快速上升。

B) 如今希望有时间娱乐的人越来越多，这是因为服务质量在迅速提高了。

C) 如今人们有了更多的闲暇时间，因而对各种服务的需求增长得如此快。

D) 如今人们有了更多的空闲时间，这就是要求迅速提高服务质量的原因。

E) 如今人们的时间更多了，这是因为服务质量在迅速地提高。

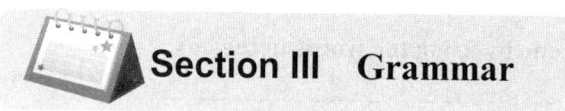

Section III Grammar

Attributive Clause（定语从句）

定语从句是指在复合句中，修饰某一名词或代词的从句。定语从句所修饰的词，叫先行词（antecedent），定语从句通常放在先行词的后面。引导定语从句的关联词有关系代词 that,

79

which, who（宾格 whom，所有格 whose）和关系副词 where, when, why 等。关系代词或关系副词放在先行词和定语从句之间，起联系作用，同时又充当定语从句的一个成分。

Review and Practice

VII. There are 10 incomplete sentences below. For each one, there are four choices marked A, B, C and D. You should choose the best answer.

1. I know the reason _____ she was so angry.
   A) that   B) which   C) how   D) why

2. I never heard such stories _____ he tells.
   A) what   B) that   C) as   D) which

3. This is the book for _____ you asked.
   A) which   B) that   C) what   D) where

4. I think it is you _____ should prove to me.
   A) that   B) which   C) who   D) whose

5. I knew her father for the simplest, hardest working man _____ ever drew the breath of life.
   A) who   B) that   C) how   D) which

6. Li Lei is the boy _____ spoken English is the best in our class.
   A) whose   B) who   C) who's   D) that

7. On the day _____ we left home there came a snowstorm.
   A) when   B) which   C) after   D) before

8. He has reached the point _____ a change is needed.
   A) that   B) which   C) where   D) when

9. What is the name of the boy _____ brought us the letter.
   A) that   B) who   C) whose   D) which

10. Once more I am in Boston, _____ I have not been for ten years.
    A) where   B) which   C) that   D) when

VIII. Please connect the two sentences into one by using the words in the box.

which	that	whose	when	where

1. Here is the girl.
   The girl's school bag has been stolen.

2. That's the science museum.
   We visited the science museum last year.

   _____

3. She still remembers the days.
   She was in the country as she was young.

   _____

4. After living in Beijing for forty years she returned to the small town.
   She grew up as a child in the small town.

   _____

5. You can borrow any book in our school library.
   You want to read the book.

   _____

Section IV Writing

Certificates (证明)

There are different kinds of certificates such as working experience certificate, doctor's certificate, income declaration which is used to certify one's true condition of identity (study experience, marital status and health condition, etc.). The form of writing a certificate is the same as writing a letter. But the receiver's name, address and ending words are often ignored. It often begins with "To Whom It May Concern" which refers to the responsible man, but it can be ignored, too. It requires brief and accurate to write a certificate.

Sample

Income Declaration

This is to certify that our company staff, XXX who hails from Suining City, Sichuan Province, I/C NO. 510902xxx, has been working in Central Hospital in Suining for 5 years since 2007. At present, he is the principal physician in the Department of Stomatology of our hospital. XXX's recent 5 years' incomes are as follows:

Year	Monthly Salary	Annual Salary

Contact Person
Signature
Position

Telephone:
Address: Central Hospital in Suining
Deshen Road, Suining City, Sichuan Province.

IX. Write a certificate.

兹证明病人李丽女士，女，27岁，因患急性阑尾炎，于2015年1月14日住院。经手术和十天治疗后，现已痊愈，将于2015年1月24日出院。建议在家休息一个星期后再上班工作。

主治医生：王志

2015 年 1 月 24 日

Section V Enjoy Yourselves

Chinese Term

Hi-tech Cheating

China targets hi-tech cheating before college entrance exam: As millions of Chinese students are doing some last-minute cramming for the upcoming national college entrance examination, authorities have launched a crackdown on sales of high-tech devices that might be used to cheat on the tests.

Unit Six   History

➤ Warm-up Question

How much do you know about American History?

Section I   Listening & Speaking

◆ Listening

Task 1.

Directions: In this section, you will hear 6 short conversations. At the end of each conversation, a question will be asked about what was said. Both the conversation and the question will be spoken twice. After each question there will be a pause. During the pause you must read the four choices marked A), B), C) and D), and decide which is the best answer. Then mark your answer.

Example:
You will hear:
M: Is it possible for you to work late, Miss Green?
W: Work late? I suppose so, if you really think it's necessary.
Q: Where does the conversation most probably take place?

You will read:
A) At the office.
B) In the waiting room.
C) At the airport.
D) In a restaurant.

From the conversation we know that the two were talking about some work they had to finish in the evening. This is most likely to have taken place at the office. Therefore, A) "At the office" is the best answer. You should choose answer A).

Sample Answer

A)   B)   C)   D)

New Words and Expressions

kindergarten ['kɪndəgɑ:tn]   *n.* 学前班；幼儿园

get caught in   遇到；碰到

Now let us listen to 6 short conversations, both the conversation and the question will be spoken twice.

1. A) When she was in university.   B) When she was in primary school.
   C) When she was in secondary school.   D) When she was in kindergarten.
2. A) Because they can back home early.   B) Because they may get caught in the traffic.
   C) Because they will have a good view.   D) Because the woman doesn't want to go.
3. A) Abraham Lincoln.   B) George Washington.
   C) Woodrow Wilson.   D) Franklin D. Roosevelt.
4. A) Lily loves her history teacher very much. B) Lily didn't enjoy studying history.
   C) Lily was interested in studying history.   D) Lily has ever studied history.
5. A) Africa.   B) Europe.
   C) Asia.   D) North Pacific.
6. A) It's terrible.   B) It's rainy.
   C) It's warm.   D) It's cloudy.

Task 2.

Directions: In this section, you will hear a short passage. At the end of the passage, you will hear two questions. Both the passage and the questions will be spoken twice. After you hear one question, you must choose the best answer from the four choices marked A), B), C) and D). Then mark your answer.

New Words and Expressions

racial ['reɪʃl]   *a.* 种族的；存在或发生于种族之间的

harmony ['hɑ:mənɪ]   *n.* 和谐；协调；融洽

Unit Six　History

race [reɪs]　　n. 种族；人种；比赛
　　　　　　　 v. 竞赛；全速行进
★applaud [əˈplɔːd]　v. 喝彩；鼓掌；称赞
◆ethnic [ˈeθnɪk]　a. 种族的，部落的，民族的
tension [ˈtenʃn]　n. 紧张局势（或关系、状况）
dream of　梦见，梦想，渴望

1. A) 1963.
   B) 1936.
   C) 1836.
   D) 1863.
2. A) Indians.
   B) Immigrants.
   C) Europeans.
   D) Africans.

Task 3.

A. **Directions: In this section, you will hear a passage three times. Listen carefully during the first reading. Then listen to the passage again. When it is being read the second time, you should fill in the ten blanks numbered from S1) to S10) with the exact words or phrases you have just heard. Finally, when the passage is read for the third time, you should check what you have written.**

New Words and Expressions

◆segregation [ˌsegrɪˈgeɪʃn]　n. 种族隔离；分开；隔离
◆spectrum [ˈspektrəm]　n. 光谱；声谱；波谱；范围
◆prejudice [ˈpredʒudɪs]　v. 对……有偏见；伤害
★minority [maɪˈnɒrətɪ]　n. 少数；少数派；少数民族
◆interracial [ˌɪntəˈreɪʃl]　a. 异族的；不同种族的
Constitution　宪法
Supreme Court　最高法院

　　The end of the Civil War finally brought **S1)** _____ to the slaves in 1865, but the blacks still had a lower position in society. The Civil Rights Movement in the 1950s and 1960s helped black people **S2)** _____ many of the rights promised in the Constitution. A 1954 Supreme Court decision ruled that segregation **S3)** _____ in public schools. **S4)** _____, American education became fairer. **S5)** _____ the gains of the Civil Rights Movement, racial problems still **S6)** _____. The laws have changed, but some people—on all sides of the color spectrum—remain **S7)** _____. Even so, in the past 40 years, race relations in America have greatly improved. **S8)** _____ groups now have equal **S9)** _____ in many areas of education, employment and housing. Interracial marriages are becoming more accepted. Maybe Dr. King's dream will **S10)** _____ after all.

B. Listen to the passage again and then decide whether each of the following statements is true (T) or false (F).

1. (   ) The social position of the blacks had been much stepped up after the Civil War.
2. (   ) There were no racial problems after the Civil Rights Movement.
3. (   ) Interracial marriages were not acceptable in the 1950s and 1960s.
4. (   ) Dr. King's dream will never be realized.

◆ **Speaking**

Task 1. Talk about your opinions on history studies.

Task 2. Two students are in pair to make a conversation as the following sample.

Sample

John: Are you interested in history?

Bob: Yes, I am. I enjoyed studying it at school, though I had trouble remembering all the dates, and my teacher never gave me good marks.

John: I love history, but I've always thought that learning the reasons behind events is more important than remembering exactly when they happened.

Bob: I wish you had been my history teacher! I might have got better marks!

John: Some people say that history repeats itself.

Bob: What does that mean? The same events never happen twice, do they?

John: The idea is that the people and dates change, but the reason why things happen stays the same.

Bob: I see. I think I'd agree with that statement. People often seem to make the same mistakes over and over again.

Section II Passage One

150th Anniversary of the U.S. Civil War

This month marks the 150th anniversary of the beginning of the U.S. Civil War—a conflict that nearly tore the United States apart. Eleven southern states seceded from the Union and formed the Confederate States of America, vowing to maintain their economic system based on agriculture and slavery.

On April 12, 1861, Confederate soldiers fired on Union troops at Fort Sumter in South Carolina. After four years of bloody battles, the Confederates surrendered.

Today, the war between the States still resonates with Americans, and in some ways, the nation is still healing from that division.

Well over a half million Americans died during the Civil War, the equivalent of losing two percent of the population. "You can imagine the impact that this would have on the whole communities throughout the country," says Ray Brown, chief of interpretation for Manassas National Battlefield Park.

Yale historian David Blight, one of the leading experts on the Civil War, says the United States reunited after the war "by finding the mutuality of sacrifice between the two sides." "What we did in this country is we suppressed having to talk about what caused that war or what its results or legacies were, focusing largely on honoring the soldier," says Blight.

He says that we shouldn't forget the military history. "But this time, we need to put the story of emancipation at the center of this narrative, because what really transformed the United States, were not those battles. What really transformed the United States was the process by which 4 million slaves were freed that necessitated a redrafting of our Constitution."

Following the War, three amendments were added to the Constitution. The 13th amendment abolished slavery forever. The 14th granted citizenship to anyone born in the United States and guaranteed equal protection to all citizens. And the 15th amendment guaranteed all citizens the right to vote.

Today, with an African-American in the White House, we have come a long way, but the legacies of the war are still being debated.

(Words 335)

（Excerpted from http://www.34en.com/Item/Show.asp?m=1&d=5246）

New Words（★三级词汇 ◆超纲词汇）

★anniversary [ˌænɪˈvɜːsərɪ]　　*n*. 周年；周年纪念

★conflict [ˈkɒnflɪkt]　　*n*. 冲突；抵触
　　　　　　　　　　　　v. 战斗；争执

◆secede [sɪˈsiːd]　　*v*. 脱离；退出

◆confederate [kənˈfedərət]　　*a*. 联盟的；同盟的；邦联的
　　　　　　　　　　　　　　　n. 同伙；合谋者；同党

◆vow [vaʊ]　　*v*. 起誓；发誓；郑重宣告
　　　　　　　　n. 誓言；郑重宣布；许愿

agriculture [ˈæɡrɪkʌltʃə(r)]　　*n*. 农业

★slavery [ˈsleɪvərɪ]　　*n*. 蓄奴制；奴隶制度；奴隶身份

★troop [truːp]　　*n*. 军队；部队；一群；一队

surrender [səˈrendə(r)]　　*v*. 投降；放弃
　　　　　　　　　　　　　n. 放弃；屈服；投降

◆resonate [ˈrezəneɪt]　　*v*. 产生回声、共鸣或共振

◆heal [hiːl]　　*v*. 愈合；治愈；（使）结束；消除

division [dɪˈvɪʒn]　　*n*. 分裂；分开；分配；除（法）

★equivalent [ɪˈkwɪvələnt]　　*a*. 相当的；相等的；等值的
　　　　　　　　　　　　　　n. 相等物

★interpretation [ɪnˌtɜːprɪˈteɪʃn]　　*n*. 翻译；口译；解释；说明

historian [hɪˈstɔːrɪən]　　*n*. 历史学家；史学工作者

expert [ˈekspɜːt]　　*a*. 熟练的；内行的

n. 专家；能手
◆mutuality [ˌmjuːtʃuˈæləti] *n.* 相互关系；相关
◆suppress [səˈpres] *v.* 禁止发表；抑制；压制；镇压
military [ˈmɪlɪtəri] *a.* 军事的，军用的
◆emancipation [ɪˌmænsɪˈpeɪʃn] *n.* （从束缚、支配下）解放
★narrative [ˈnærətɪv] *n.* 故事；记叙文；叙述；讲述
transform [trænsˈfɔːm] *v.* 改变；改造；改革
necessitate [nəˈsesɪteɪt] *v.* 使……成为必要，需要
★amend [əˈmend] *v.* 修正；修订
★amendment [əˈmendmənt] *n.* 修正；修订
◆abolish [əˈbɒlɪʃ] *v.* 废除；废止
★grant [grɑːnt] *n.* 拨款
v. 授予；同意；准予

Phrases and Expressions

tear apart 使……分裂；把……痛苦地分开；把……弄乱
well over 多余；超过
focus on 致力于；集中于
come a long way 取得进展；明显提高

Proper Names

the Confederate States of America 美利坚邦联；美利坚（南方）联盟
Fort Sumter 萨姆特堡（位于美国南卡罗来纳州查尔斯顿港的一处石制防御工事，始建于 1827 年，以美国独立战争英雄托马斯·萨姆特将军的姓来命名。）
South Carolina 南卡罗来纳（美国）
Manassas National Battlefield Park 马纳萨斯国家内战公园
Yale 耶鲁大学 (=Yale University)

Read and Think

I. Answer the following questions according to the passage.

1. How long did the U.S. Civil War last?
2. What is Americans' specific concern regarding the U.S. Civil War?
3. What really transformed the United States according to Blight's opinion?

Read and Try

II. Fill in each blank with a right word in its right form using the words in the following box.

| grant | surrender | guarantee | conflict |
| transform | amend | sacrifice | equivalent |

1. I will rather die than _____.
2. If so, your points of view are bound to _____ with the professor's.
3. After he criticized me, I took pains to _____.
4. We regret being unable to _____ you the 25% discount you desire.
5. Silence is sometimes _____ to agreement.
6. The prince _____ into a frog in the story.
7. He earned money at the _____ of his health.
8. This watch is _____ for two years.

III. There are eight incomplete sentences below. For each sentence, there are four choices marked A, B, C and D. You should choose the proper one to complete each sentence.

1. The little boy tried to _____ the phone book.
   A) tear down   B) tear into   C) tear away   D) tear apart
2. _____ caused the accident is still a complete mystery.
   A) What   B) That   C) How   D) Where
3. Here is my car _____ I go to work.
   A) where   B) by which   C) from which   D) in which
4. Your proposal would _____ changing our plans.
   A) necessitate   B) necessary   C) necessitous   D) necessarily
5. Some diseases are _____ by certain water animals.
   A) transplanted   B) transported   C) transformed   D) transmitted
6. The enemy was forced to make an unconditional _____.
   A) giving up   B) quit   C) surrender   D) desert
7. He was _____ his freedom on the condition that he left the country.
   A) giving   B) given   C) granting   D) granted
8. The _____ between them seems ceaseless.
   A) confirm   B) conflict   C) confuse   D) confect

Read and Translate

IV. Translate the following sentences into English.

1. 自 20 世纪 70 年代以来，电脑技术有了很大的发展。(come a long way)
2. 她的全部精力都花在了孩子们身上。(focus on)
3. 就连你所能想到的最壮的人也不能光用手就将木头撕裂。(tear apart)
4. 实际上，这使得经济更加稳定。(add to)

Reading Skills

Retaining Concepts and Organizing Facts

Efficient reading demands more than simply remembering facts. It requires the reader to retain concepts and organize facts. A conscious reader must combine facts and ideas mentally, make generalizations, and gain greater insight and deeper understanding from all his reading. Writers often organize their supporting details according to some particular pattern, and their thoughts are developed logically.

Directions: Read the following paragraphs carefully, and then choose the best answer.

Passage One

On July 4, 1776, the Continental Congress approved the Declaration of Independence. Later, people in New York City heard about the Declaration when George Washington brought it to his troops. Then, when they heard the news, New Yorkers tore down a statue of King George III. After that, the statue was melted down and made into bullets. These were used to shoot at the British troops.

(Words 66)

1. The author organizes the details of this paragraph according to _____.

    A) order of importance B) spatial development
    C) time order D) comparison and contrast

Passage Two

In recent decades, cities have grown so large that now about 50% of the Earth's population lives in urban areas. There are several reasons for this occurrence. First, the increasing industrialization of the nineteenth century resulted in the creation of many factory jobs, which tended to be located in cities. These jobs, with their promise of a better material life, attracted many people from rural areas. Second, there were many schools established to educate the children of the new factory laborers. The promise of a better education persuaded many families to leave farming communities and move to the cities. Finally, as the cities grew, people established places of leisure, entertainment, and culture, such as sports stadiums, theaters, and museums. For many people, these facilities made city life appear more interesting than life on the farm, and therefore drew them away from rural communities.

(Words 143)

2. The author arranges the topic sentence and supporting details according to _____.

   A) spatial development   B) cause and effect
   C) comparison and contrast   D) time order

   Passage Three

   Life in the city is quite different from life in the suburb. People living in the city are constantly exposed to the hustle and bustle of urban life. But life in the suburb is generally quiet and casual and generally more low-key than in the city. If city dwellers want to see trees and grass, they must go to one of the public parks. On the other hand, the streets of many suburban communities are lined with trees and shrubs, and each house has its own grassy yard. A person living in the city is close to many sources of entertainment, but people living in suburban areas must go into the city for entertainment.

(Words 118)

3. What kind of life is generally more low-key? _____.

   A) Life in the city   B) Life in the suburbs
   C) Life in urban areas   D) Not mentioned

   Passage Four

   The kitchen was in a mess. Along the left wall were the counter and sink covered with dirty dishes and garbage. On the far wall the washing machine groaned under a load of filthy clothes. Right next to the door where I was standing, on my right, I saw old newspapers, an overturned catsup bottle, and a wet, half-eaten hot dog. At the far end of the right wall the refrigerator stood with the door ajar and milk dripping down from the top shelf. It was the messiest kitchen I had ever seen.

(Words 96)

4. According to the passage, where was the author standing? _____.

   A) At the far end of the right wall
   B) Next to the door
   C) At the far end of the left wall
   D) In the living room

Section II Passage Two

American History Lessons

American history is taught to students at all levels of education, from elementary school to junior school to senior school. Aside from reading textbooks, students take trips to museums, watch movies and programs about historical topics, and write research reports.

School children are taught both the good and bad aspects of American history. For example, slavery is talked about openly and honestly. So the Native Americans were badly treated during the expansion of America.

America was founded by immigrants from Europe. It now includes immigrants from all over the world. It is now customary to refer to American Indians as "Native Americans". Also, Black Americans are referred to as "African Americans." This linguistic change reflects the cultural heritage and background of these groups.

American children study very little Asian history. There are world history classes required at every level of public education, but those courses tend to be very general.

At the university level, there are a wide range of classes. Lower level history and literature courses include textbooks, works of literature, and other documents translated into English. Advanced level courses include materials in their original languages. Popular areas of focus include Chinese, Japanese and Indian history and literature.

Recently, several classics of Eastern philosophy have become very popular. In particular, the *Dao De Jing* and *Bhagavad-Gita* are available in many translations. Classics of literature, such as *Dream of the Red Chamber* and *Journey to the West* are also easily found. Asian martial arts also have a large number of enthusiasts in America. Arts such as Tai Kwan Do, Judo, Aikido and Kung Fu attract people of all ages. Tai Chi Chuan is also practiced by those interested in Asian arts and medicine.

(Words 285)

(Excerpted from *American History* Lessons)

New Words（★三级词汇 ◆超纲词汇）

  expansion [ɪkˈspænʃn]   *n.* 扩张；膨胀；扩大
◆customary [ˈkʌstəmərɪ]   *a.* 习惯的；习俗的；通常的
  reflect [rɪˈflekt]   *v.* 体现；反映；反射；反省
  heritage [ˈherɪtɪdʒ]   *n.* 遗产；继承物；传统
  range [reɪndʒ]   *n.* 范围；幅度；距离；一系列
        v. 延伸；（在某范围内）变化
  advanced [ədˈvɑːnst]   *a.* 高级的；先进的
★original [əˈrɪdʒənl]   *a.* 原始的；最初的；独创的；新颖的
★philosophy [fəˈlɒsəfɪ]   *n.* 哲学；人生哲学；主旨
◆martial [ˈmɑːʃl]   *a.* 武术的；军事的
  enthusiast [ɪnˈθjuːzɪæst]   *n.* 爱好者；热衷者；热心人

Phrases and Expressions

aside from   除……之外；既……又……
refer to...as...   把……称为；认为……是
tend to   往往会；倾向于；易于
translate into   （把……）翻译成……；把……转化成
in particular   特别；尤其

Proper Names

Native Americans   美国土著居民
Bhagavad-Gita《薄伽梵歌》
Dream of the Red Chamber《红楼梦》
Journey to the West《西游记》
Tai Kwan Do   跆拳道
Judo   柔道

Unit Six　History

Aikido　合气道
Kung Fu　中国功夫
Tai Chi Chuan　太极拳

Read and Choose

V. There are five questions or unfinished statements in the following. For each of them there are four choices marked A, B, C and D. Decide the best answer according to Passage Two.

1. How does an American study American history?
   A) Reading textbooks.
   B) Taking trips to museums.
   C) Watching movies and programs about historical topics.
   D) All of the above.

2. Who are the first immigrants in America?
   A) Europeans.
   B) Asians.
   C) Africans.
   D) Latinos.

3. Which is not included in lower level history and literature courses?
   A) Textbooks.
   B) Materials in their original languages.
   C) Documents translated into English.
   D) Works of literature.

4. Which classic of Eastern philosophy is very popular in America according to the passage?
   A) Tale of Genji.
   B) Dream of the Red Chamber.
   C) Journey to the West.
   D) Dao De Jing.

5. Which of the following statements is true according to the passage?
   A) School children are only taught the bad aspects of American history.
   B) American children never study Asian history.
   C) Dream of the Red Chamber is available in many translations.
   D) Popular areas of focus include Chinese, Japanese and Korea history and literature.

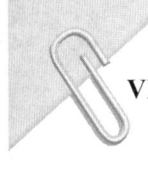
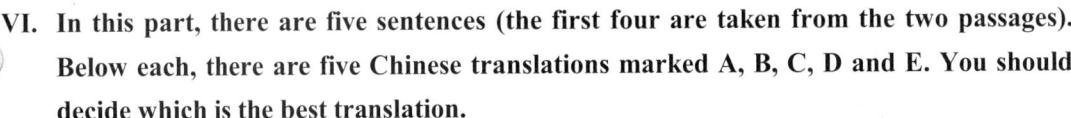

VI. In this part, there are five sentences (the first four are taken from the two passages). Below each, there are five Chinese translations marked A, B, C, D and E. You should decide which is the best translation.

1. What really transformed the United States was the process by which 4 million slaves were freed that necessitated a redrafting of our Constitution. *(Passage One)*
   A) 400万奴隶自由后，获得了权利，也就转变了美国修改宪法的进程。
   B) 真正改变美国的是400万奴隶自由的历程，从而使得我们重新起草了宪法。
   C) 真正使美国转变的是这些400万奴隶解放了，使宪法重新修改的过程。
   D) 真正改变美国的是400万奴隶被解放的过程，从而使得我们修改了宪法。
   E) 真正改变美国的是400万奴隶获救的历史，从而我们能修改宪法。

2) The 14th granted citizenship to anyone born in the United States and guaranteed equal protection to all citizens. *(Passage One)*
   A) 任何出生在美国的人都有第十四种公民身份，委托他们去保证公民的合法权利。
   B) 第十四条例规定授予所有在美国出生的人公民身份，还确保所有的人都有同等的公民权利。
   C) 第十四修正案赋予所有在美国出生的人以美国公民身份，并且确保所有的人得到平等保护。
   D) 第十四修正案授予任何在美国出生的人公民身份的荣誉，还保证每个人都得到平等的保护。
   E) 第十四修正案赋予任何在美国出生的人以美国公民身份，并且确保所有公民得到同等保护。

3. There are world history classes required at every level of public education, but those courses tend to be very general. *(Passage Two)*
   A) 尽管各水平的公立教育要求孩子上世界历史课，但那些科目都趋向于笼统化。
   B) 世界历史课在不同层次的公立学校要求下开设，但这些科目常常笼统了。
   C) 虽然不同层次的公立教育要求孩子上世界历史课，但这些课程往往过于笼统。
   D) 所有层次的公立学校要求上世界历史课，但是那些课程往往都太常见了。
   E) 有的世界历史课是要求非常普遍的，在不同层次的公立教育有不同的要求。

4. Arts such as Tai Kwan Do, Judo, Aikido and Kung Fu attract people of all ages. *(Passage Two)*
   A) 跆拳道、柔道、合气道和功夫吸引了各个年龄段的人。
   B) 诸如跆拳道、柔道、合气道和功夫的艺术品吸引了所有人。
   C) 所有的人都喜欢跆拳道、柔道、合气道和功夫这些艺术。
   D) 跆拳道、柔道、合气道和功夫对于使所有年纪的人都有魅力。
   E) 跆拳道、柔道、合气道和功夫对于所有年龄的人都是引人注目的。

5. As you have done the market survey, I would like to discuss with you the possibility of selling our products in the US.

A) 因为美国产品有市场资料，所以我们要研究开发我们产品的可能性。

B) 因为你有美国市场资料，所以我希望与你讨论美国产品的销售情况。

C) 你已经作了市场调查，所以我想和你讨论在美国销售我们产品的可能性。

D) 你已了解了市场，因此我希望能与你商讨在美国开发我们产品的可能性。

E) 由于你在市场调查过，所以我想和你讨论在美国销售我们产品的可能性。

Section III Grammar

Adverbial Clause（状语从句）

用作状语的从句叫做状语从句，引导状语从句的关联词是从属连词。状语从句同状语一样，在句中的位置比较灵活，可置于句首、句末或句中。状语从句根据其用途可分为时间状语从句、地点状语从句、原因状语从句、结果状语从句、程度状语从句、目的状语从句、条件状语从句、让步状语从句、方式状语从句等九种类型。

Review and Practice

VII. There are 10 incomplete sentences below. For each one, there are four choices marked A, B, C and D. You should choose the best answer.

1. _____ we gave him something to eat, he would save it up for his little sister.
   A) Whatever   B) However
   C) Whenever   D) Whichever

2. _____, I have to put it away and focus my attention on study this week.
   A) However the story is amusing   B) No matter amusing the story is
   C) However amusing the story is   D) No matter how the story is amusing

3. —May I go now?
   —_____ you've finished your work, you may go.
   A) After   B) Although
   C) Now that   D) As soon as

4. _____ he thought he was helping us with the work, he was actually in the way.
   A) Although   B) Unless   C) Because   D) When

5. I have been keeping the portrait _____ I can see it every day, as it always reminds me of my childhood in Paris.

   A) since   B) where   C) as   D) if

6. _____ your homework carefully, some mistakes can be avoided.

   A) Having checked   B) Check   C) If you check   D) To check

7. —Did you remember to return the book to our English teacher?

   —Yes. I gave it to him _____ I saw him.

   A) once   B) while   C) if   D) the moment

8. It will be five years _____ we meet again.

   A) since   B) until   C) before   D) when

9. Most animals have little connection with animals of a different kind, _____ they hunt them for food.

   A) if   B) while   C) unless   D) as

10. Never lose heart _____ difficulty you may meet with.

    A) what   B) whatever   C) how   D) however

VIII. Correct the errors in the following sentences.

1. As long as we are allowed to, we can't drink any beer.
2. As I admit that there are problems, I don't agree that they cannot be solved.
3. "Where my feet remain standing above the water level, there is hope." said the captain.
4. Even if you begin, I think you must continue.
5. I recognized you once I saw you at the airport.

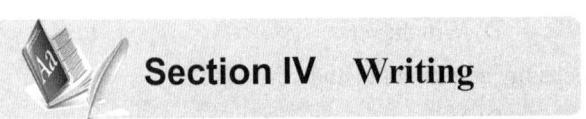

Section IV Writing

Advertisement（广告）

Advertisement is the non-person communication of information usually paid for and usually persuasive in nature about products, services or ideas by identified sponsors through the various media.

Unit Six History

Sample

> Seiko
>
> The First Ever,
>
> The Last You'll Ever Need.
>
> The first and only quartz watch to generate and store electrical energy through nature human movement.
>
> Needs no battery.
>
> Perpetually accurate, totally reliable.
>
> Environment friendly.
>
> Exclusive from Seiko.
>
> Seiko
>
> Knietic
>
> Someday all watches will be made this way.

IX. Write a wanted-advertisement for a company according to the following information.

工程管理助理

职责：

    —为重庆的工程提供服务。

    —协助工程经理处理日常事务。

    —负责文件管理，为学员和家长们提供客户服务。

要求：

    —大学及以上程度。

    —英语和计算机技能良好。

    —有过在国际机构组织中的相关工作经验。

    —耐心，细心，善于协作。具有强烈的团队工作精神。

Section V Enjoy Yourselves

Lines in the Film of "The Spy Next Door"

Nora: Mom! Jethro's eating my underwear! Here, piggy, piggy, piggy. Jethro.

Ian: Mom, before she starts, there isn't **a shred of evidence** to support her allegations.
Farren: Gillian, your son is a **psycho**. He **booby-trapped** my hair dryer.
Ian: Nice hypothesis, but you can't prove it.
Farren: Yeah, but I can hurt you. Mom! Mom! She needs to be medicated.
Nora: Come on, Jethro. Come here.
Farren: I hate this family. Come here.
Nora: Jethro, you're getting a **time out**.
Gillian: Come on, guys. **Backpack**.
Farren: What? It's **in style**.
Gillian: It's inappropriate. Go put on some jeans. And spit out the gum. So, what color do you want to wear today? Red? Blue? Purple?
Nora: Pink, Momma, pink.
Gillian: Farren.
Farren: What? You said jeans.
Gillian: I meant in your size. Come on, guys. Come on. We don't want to be late. There you go. Come on, sweetie.
Farren: No! Get out!
Gillian: No fighting.
Bob: Allow me.
Gillian: Hi. Are we still on for dinner?
Bob: I'll be there.
Gillian: **We have an audience**.
Farren: Yuck. I'm going to vomit.
Ian: He is such a loser.
Nora: I like Bob. He's nice.
Farren: He's a boring pen importer. He does the same routine every day. He's like a robot.
Ian: That's 'cause he is a robot. A **cyborg**, sent from the future, to destroy humanity. Starting with us.
Gillian: Well, it's been three months. Happy anniversary. What is it?
Bob: I have to tell you about my job. This might shock you, but you should know everything before this relationship goes further.
Gillian: Don't, Bob.
Bob: What?
Gillian: I'm very happy when I'm with you. No one has ever made me laugh like you do, and if I were a single woman, I could see a real future for us. But I'm a **package deal**.

Bob: What do you mean?

Gillian: My kids are my priority and... How can I put this gently?

Bob: They hate me.

Gillian: Yeah.

Bob: I can make them like me. See?

Gillian: See? You can't make kids like you, not mine or anyone's. My kids have been through a lot, and... I don't think we should take the next step until they **warm up to you**.

Bob: Doesn't your happiness count? Excuse me. Sorry, I gotta go. Emergency at work.

Gillian: **No ink**?

Bob: It's much bigger. Sorry, really. I will explain everything tomorrow.

Gillian: Okay. I'll see you tomorrow.

1. a shred of evidence：丝毫的证据。也可以说成是 a shred of truth，not a shred of evidence 就是说"没有丝毫的证据表明……"。

2. psycho：神经病。Farren 在这里是说"你儿子发什么神经？"

3. booby-trap：设陷阱，布置机关。也可以指安放饵雷。例如：The car had been booby-trapped by terrorists.（恐怖分子在那辆汽车里安放了饵雷。）

4. time out：工作中的休息时间，也可以指比赛时的暂停。而 out of time 则用来表示"不合时宜"，例如：He is born out of time.（他生不逢时。）

5. backpack：背包，背包旅行。背着旅行包去长途旅行的驴友就称为 backpacker（背包客），这种旅行方式也称为 go backpacking。登山者或远足者使用的背包、旅行包就是 rucksack。

6. in style：时髦，别具风格。此外，in style 还可以表示"很成功"，或者场面非常"豪华、隆重"，常用 in great/grand style 来形容。例如：If ever she gives a party she likes to do it in style.（她每举办舞会，总喜欢搞得很排场。）

7. We have an audience：Gillian 在这里的意思是"孩子们正盯着我们"。

8. cyborg：科幻故事中的电子人、半机械人。

9. package deal：一揽子交易，整批处理。Gillian 在这里是说"我还要带小不点"。
此外，package deal 还可以表示"成套服务"，例如：I want a package deal including airfare and hotel.（我需要一个成套服务，包括机票和住宿。）

10. warm up to someone/something: to become more fervent and earnest toward someone, something, or a group; to become more responsive and receptive to someone, a group, or something.（对某人、某事或某团体更加热情、真挚，更容易接受）
    例如：After we talked, he began to warm up to us a little.
    在我们交谈后，他开始有些接受我了。

11. no ink: 无语了，没话说了。

Unit Seven Literature

➢ Warm-up Question

Are you interested in English literature? Do you know any famous works of English literature?

Section I Listening & Speaking

◆ Listening

Task 1.

Directions: In this section, you will hear 6 short conversations. At the end of each conversation, a question will be asked about what was said. Both the conversation and the question will be spoken twice. After each question there will be a pause. During the pause you must read the four choices marked A), B), C) and D), and decide which is the best answer. Then mark your answer.

Example:
You will hear:
M: Is it possible for you to work late, Miss Green?
W: Work late? I suppose so, if you really think it's necessary.
Q: Where does the conversation most probably take place?

You will read:
A) At the office.
B) In the waiting room.
C) At the airport.
D) In a restaurant.

From the conversation we know that the two were talking about some work they had to finish in the evening. This is most likely to have taken place at the office. Therefore, A) "At the office" is the best answer. You should choose answer A).

Sample Answer

~~A)~~   B)   C)   D)

Now let us listen to 6 short conversations, both the conversation and the question will be spoken twice.

1. A) Helen Keller's.   B) Helen Kate's.
   C) Henry's.   D) Three Days to See.
2. A) Gone with the Wind.   B) A Tale of Two Cities.
   C) Pride and Prejudice.   D) The Merchant of Venice.
3. A) She is the 20th woman who got the Nobel Prize in literature.
   B) She is the 12th woman who got the Nobel Prize in literature.
   C) She is not a German.
   D) She got the Nobel Prize in 2008.
4. A) Martin Armstrong.   B) William Shakespeare.
   C) Sarah Austin.   D) John Donne.
5. A) The woman was late again.   B) The woman's car was broken down.
   C) The man disliked the woman.   D) The woman felt angry.
6. A) He has a headache.   B) He has a bad cough.
   C) He has a cold.   D) He needs a rest.

Task 2.

Directions: In this section, you will hear a short passage. At the end of the passage, you will hear two questions. Both the passage and the questions will be spoken twice. After you hear one question, you must choose the best answer from the four choices marked A), B), C) and D). Then mark your answer.

New Words and Expressions

   enjoyable [ɪnˈdʒɔɪəbl]   *a.* 令人快乐的；使人愉快的

★acquire [əˈkwaɪə]   *v.* 获得；得到；取得

◆extract [ɪkˈstrækt]   *v.* 取出；拔出；摘录；选录
          [ˈekstrækt]   *n.* 榨取物；摘录；选录

   instruction [ɪnˈstrʌkʃn]   *n.* 传授；教导；指令；用法说明

◆tedium ['tiːdɪəm] *n.* 单调乏味；冗长

◆resignation [ˌrezɪɡ'neɪʃn] *n.* 辞职；辞呈

◆alacrity [ə'lækrətɪ] *n.* 欣然同意；乐意

get through 设法做或完成某事

1. A) The author thinks reading should be enjoyable.

   B) The author thinks reading should be useful for passing the examinations.

   C) The author thinks reading should be helpful for acquiring information.

   D) The author thinks reading is tedium.

2. A) Reading can bring the reader a degree.

   B) Reading can help the reader earn a living.

   C) Reading can help the reader live more fully if he enjoys reading them.

   D) Reading can help the reader live more fully without enjoying them.

Task 3.

A. **Directions:** In this section, you will hear a passage three times. Listen carefully during the first reading. Then listen to the passage again. When it is being read the second time, you should fill in the ten blanks numbered from S1) to S10) with the exact words or phrases you have just heard. Finally, when the passage is read for the third time, you should check what you have written.

New Words and Expressions

★genius ['dʒiːnɪəs] *n.* 天才；创造力

◆outrageous [aʊt'reɪdʒəs] *a.* 骇人的；无法容忍的；令人惊讶的

◆peculiarly [pɪ'kjuːlɪəlɪ] *ad.* 很；不寻常地；特别

★innocent ['ɪnəsnt] *a.* 清白的；无罪的；无知的；没有恶意的

◆metaphor ['metəfə] *n.* 隐喻；暗喻

◆drawling ['drɔːlɪŋ] *a.* 慢吞吞的

◆rhythm ['rɪðəm] *n.* 节奏；节奏感

tall tale *n.* 无稽之谈；荒诞不经的故事

◆prose style 散文体

matter-of-fact 实事求是的

Mark Twain was the first **S1)** _____ American writer to be **S2)** _____ away from the East

Unit Seven   Literature

Coast. He grew up in a small **S3)** _____ on the banks of the Mississippi River and received only a basic public school **S4)** _____. He began working in a printer's shop when he was still a boy, and this **S5)** _____ led to a series of newspaper jobs in the Midwest and the West. Twain was a new voice, an **S6)** _____ genius, a man of the people, and he quickly won readers. He captured a peculiarly American **S7)** _____ of humor, telling outrageous **S8)** _____ and tall tales in a calm, innocent, matter-of-fact **S9)** _____. He sometimes used local dialect for comic effect, but even his normal prose style sounded distinctively American—rich in metaphor, newly **S10)** _____ words and drawling rhythms.

B. Listen to the passage again and then decide whether each of the following statements is true (T) or false (F).

1. (   ) Mark Twain was the first American writer to be born away from the East Coast.
2. (   ) Mark Twain grew up in a small town on the banks of the Mississippi River and received a higher education there.
3. (   ) Mark Twain captured a peculiarly American sense of humor.
4. (   ) Mark Twain sometimes used local dialect for comic effect.

◆ **Speaking**

Task 1. Talk about your favorite book with your partner.

Task 2. Two students are in a pair to make a conversation as the following sample.

Sample

David: Oh! This book is fantastic. Do you want to have a look?
Li: Really, which book? Who wrote it?
David: It's Margaret Mitchell's famous works *Gone with the Wind*.
Li: Oh! I have heard a lot about it, but no chance to see it; can you lend it to me after you read it?
David: Of course. I really love the heroine—she is beautiful, brave and intelligent.
Li: I can't even wait now!
David: I'll finish it tonight, and you can get it tomorrow.
Li: That's great. Thanks!
David: You're welcome!

Section II Passage One

Three Days to See

All of us have read thrilling stories in which the hero had only a limited and specified time to live. Sometimes it was as long as a year, sometimes as short as 24 hours. But always we were interested in discovering just how the doomed hero chose to spend his last days or his last hours. I speak, of course, of free men who have a choice, not condemned criminals whose sphere of activities is strictly delimited.

Such stories set us thinking, wondering what we should do under similar circumstances. What events, what experiences, what associations should we crowd into those last hours as mortal beings, what regrets?

Sometimes I have thought it would be an excellent rule to live each day as if we should die tomorrow. Such an attitude would emphasize sharply the values of life. We should live each day with gentleness, vigor and a keenness of appreciation which are often lost when time stretches before us in the constant panorama of more days and months and years to come. There are those, of course, who would adopt the Epicurean motto of "Eat, drink, and be merry". But most people would be chastened by the certainty of impending death.

In stories the doomed hero is usually saved at the last minute by some stroke of fortune, but almost always his sense of values is changed. He becomes more appreciative of the meaning of life and its permanent spiritual values. It has often been noted that those who live, or have lived, in the shadow of death bring a mellow sweetness to everything they do.

Most of us, however, take life for granted. We know that one day we must die, but usually we picture that day as far in the future. When we are in buoyant health, death is all but unimaginable. We seldom think of it. The days stretch out in an endless vista. So we go about our petty tasks, hardly aware of our listless attitude toward life.

The same lethargy, I am afraid, characterizes the use of all our faculties and senses. Only the deaf appreciate hearing, only the blind realize the manifold blessings that lie in sight. Particularly does this observation apply to those who have lost sight and hearing in adult life. But those who have never suffered impairment of sight or hearing seldom make the fullest use of these blessed faculties. Their eyes and ears take in all sights and sounds hazily, without concentration and with little appreciation. It is the same old story of not being grateful for what we have until we lose it, of not being conscious of health until we are ill.

I have often thought it would be a blessing if each human being was stricken blind and deaf for a few days at some time during his early adult life. Darkness would make him more appreciative of sight; silence would teach him the joys of sound.

(Words 491）

（Excerpted from http://www.tingclass.net/show-8441-241166-1.html）

New Words（★三级词汇 ◆超纲词汇）

◆thrilling ['θrɪlɪŋ]　*a.* 惊心动魄的；使人激动的；毛骨悚然的
★specify ['spesɪfaɪ]　*v.* 指定；详细说明
◆doom [dum；du:m]　*n.* 死亡；毁灭；劫数
　　　　　　　　　　 v. 注定某人（死亡、毁灭、失败等）
◆criminal ['krɪmɪnl]　*n.* 罪犯，犯人
　　　　　　　　　　 a. 犯罪的，刑事上的
　condemned [kən'demd]　*a.* 已被定罪的
★sphere [sfɪə(r)]　*n.*（某人的活动、兴趣、影响等的）范围；球，球体
◆mortal ['mɔ:tl]　*a.* 终有一死的；有深仇大恨的；不共戴天的
　vigor ['vɪɡə(r)]　*n.* 体力；精力；活力
◆keenness [ki:nes]　*n.* 敏锐
★stretch [stretʃ]　*n.* 一段时间，一段路程；伸展，扩张
　　　　　　　　　 v. 拉伸；伸展
◆panorama [ˌpænə'rɑ:mə]　*n.* 风景的全貌
◆impending [ɪm'pendɪŋ]　*a.* 即将发生的；迫在眉睫的
★permanent ['pɜ:mənənt]　*a.* 永久性的，耐久的，固定不变的
　mellow ['meləʊ]　*a.* 熟透的；芳醇的；(人格、思想等)老练的，成熟的；
◆buoyant ['bɔɪənt]　*a.* 轻快的，活泼的;（指物体）能漂浮的；有浮力的
◆lethargy ['leθədʒɪ]　*n.* 昏睡；倦怠；无精打采
★faculty ['fækltɪ]　*n.* 才能，能力；大学的系，科，院；全体从业人员
◆manifold ['mænɪfəʊld]　*a.* 繁多的，多种的；多方面的；多种形式的
◆impairment [ɪm'peəmənt]　*n.* 故障，缺陷；损害，损伤

Phrases and Expressions

crowd into　大批涌入（某狭小空间）

take sb./sth. for granted 因熟悉某人 (某事物) 而觉察不出真正价值；认为理当如此
all but 几乎，差不多
stretch out (使某事物) 延续或足够所需

Proper Names

  Epicurean 伊壁鸠鲁学说的。伊壁鸠鲁(Epicurus)，古希腊哲学家，他认为生活的主要目的是享乐，而终极的享受只有通过合理的生活，比如节制自己的欲望等才能达到。而后世将生活享乐这一目的过分强调，却忽视了他所强调的达此目的的手段，所以伊壁鸠鲁的信徒一词已经具有贬义，用来形容那些追求享乐的人们。他有一句名言常常为人所引用："吃喝享乐吧，因为也许明天你就会死去(Eat, Drink and be Merry, for tomorrow you may die)。"

Read and Think

I. **Answer the following questions according to the passage.**
1. According to the author, what were people always interested in about the doomed hero?
2. According to the author, what would be the excellent rule of life?
3. What do people think about death and life when they are in good health?
4. Why does the author think it would be a blessing if each human being were blind and deaf for a few days?

Read and Try

II. **Fill in each blank with a right word in its right form using the words in the following box.**

| thrilling | impending | sphere | permanent |
| mortal | petty | vigor | manifold |

1. The injury left him with a _____ limp.
2. The tiger in the cage gave a _____ cry.
3. All human beings are_____.
4. This is a versatile machine with _____ uses.
5. He is a young man with plenty of _____.
6. Don't bother me with these _____ problems.
7. Her _____ of interests is very limited.
8. They were unaware of the _____ danger.

III. There are eight incomplete sentences below. For each sentence, there are four choices marked A), B), C) and D). You should choose the proper one to complete each sentence.

1. He was inadequately prepared for the _____ examinations.
   A) impend   B) impending
   C) depend   D) depending
2. She is dancing with the beautiful tones of a violin under the _____ moonlight.
   A) mellow   B) mellowness
   C) follow   D) mature
3. The party was _____ but over when we arrived.
   A) many   B) all
   C) no   D) some
4. Disturbing thoughts _____ into my mind.
   A) crowding   B) has crowded
   C) crowded   D) crowds
5. If you were _____ of all that, you would change your mind.
   A) know   B) awareness
   C) knowing   D) aware
6. I always _____ it for granted that my mother did everything for me when I was young.
   A) took   B) take
   C) takes   D) taken
7. It was a _____ problem and they soon solved it.
   A) petty   B) pretty
   C) prefer   D) pity
8. Many a time as a boy _____ that hill.
   A) I have climbed   B) I have been climbed
   C) have I climbed   D) I climbed Read and Translate

Read and Translate

IV. Translate the following sentences into English.
   1. 我们大家涌进了玛丽那狭小的客厅。(crowd into)
   2. 当人们发现这些徒步旅行者的时候,他们已经累坏了,而且几乎冻僵了。(all but)
   3. 一些人觉得父母为他们付出一切是理所当然的。(take ... for granted)
   4. 受到老板的表扬之后,他用更加充沛的精力和热情工作。(vigor)

109

Reading Skills

Recognizing the Author's Attitude

Writers are not necessarily neutral or objective when they write, particularly if they are trying to persuade readers to agree with their opinions. It is important that you recognize what an author's attitude is in relation to the ideas or information being presented. This is because such attitudes can influence the ways in which information is presented.

Directions: Read the following paragraphs carefully, and then choose the best answer.

Passage One

Mr. Smith taught English at a school. At the beginning of his lesson, he liked to have one of his students give a report on any subject. When it was Jack's turn, he told his audience about his elder brother who was a local worker. But during the report, his eyes were staring at the world map on the wall all the time. Mr. Smith knew that Jack didn't look at the audience because he was nervous. He said to Jack jokingly, "We can see you miss your brother very much. But is he good now in South America?"

(Words 99)

1. The style of the passage is _____.

    A) miserable   B) sorrowful

    C) happy   D) humorous

Passage Two

Long long ago, there was a big cat in the house. He caught many mice while they were stealing food. One day the mice had a meeting to talk about the way to deal with their common enemy. Some said this, and some said that. At last a young mouse got up, and said that he had a good idea. "We could tie a bell around the neck of the cat. Then when he comes near, we can hear the sound of the bell, and run away." Everyone approved of this proposal, but an old wise mouse got up and said, "That sounds good, but who will tie the bell to the cat?" The mice looked at each other, but nobody spoke.

(Words 124)

2. The author wants to show the truth: _____.

    A) mice is very smart   B) easier said than done

    C) mice is very brave   D) cat is very fierce

Passage Three

On Tuesday August 11th, 1911, a young artist, Louis Beraud, arrived at the Louvre（卢浮宫）in Paris to complete a painting of the Salon Carre（卡雷沙龙，卢浮宫的画廊名）. This was

the room where the world's most famous painting, the Mona Lisa by Leonardo da Vinci（列奥那多·达·芬奇）, was on display. To his surprise there was an empty space where the painting should have been. At 11 o'clock the museum authorities realized that the painting had been stolen.

(Words 76)

3. According to the passage, the author tells us _____.

    A) a young artist named Louis Beraud

    B) the Mona Lisa was the world's most famous painting

    C) the Mona Lisa was drawn by Leonardo da Vinci

    D) the Mona Lisa was stolen

    Passage Four

    A lion was awakened from sleep by a mouse running over his face. Rising up angrily, he caught him and was about to kill him, when the mouse piteously entreated, saying: "If you would only spare my life, I would be sure to repay your kindness." The Lion laughed and let him go. It happened shortly after this that the Lion was caught by some hunters, who bound him with strong ropes. The Mouse, recognizing his roar, came and gnawed the rope with his teeth and set him free.

    (Words 90)

4. According to the passage, we can learn_____.

    A) the lion is proud   B) the mouse is clever

    C) the weak can help the power   D) the mouse can help the lion

Section II Passage Two

About Reading Books

Virginia Woolf

It is simple enough to say that since books have classes—fiction, biography, and poetry—we should separate them and take from each what it is right that each should give us. Yet few people ask from books what books can give us. Most commonly we come to books with blurred and divided minds, asking of fiction that it shall be true, of poetry that it shall be false, of biography that it shall be flattering, of history that it shall enforce our own prejudices. If we could banish all such preconceptions when we read, that would be an admirable beginning. Do not dictate to your author; try to become him. Be his fellow-worker and accomplice. If you hang back, and reserve and criticize at first, you are preventing yourself from getting the fullest possible value from what you read. But if you open your mind as widely as possible, then signs and hints of almost imperceptible fineness, from the twist and turn of the first sentences, will bring you into the presence of a human being unlike any other. Steep yourself in this, acquaint yourself with this, and soon you will find that your author is giving you, or attempting to give you, something far more definite. The thirty-two chapters of a novel—if we consider how to read a novel first—are an attempt to make something as formed and controlled as a building; but words are more impalpable than bricks; reading is a longer and more complicated process than seeing. Perhaps the quickest way to understand the elements of what a novelist is doing is not to read, but to write; to make your own experiment with the dangers and difficulties of words. Recall, then, some events that has left a distinct impression on you—how at the corner of the street, perhaps, you passed two people talking. A tree shook; an electric light danced; the tone of the talk was comic, but also tragic; a whole vision; an entire conception, seemed contained in that moment.

(Words 334)

（选自中国社会出版社《晨读英语美文》同名文章；作者维吉尼亚·伍尔夫）

New Words（★三级词汇 ◆超纲词汇）

　　fiction ['fɪkʃn]　　*n.* 小说；虚构的事
◆biography [baɪ'ɒgrəfɪ]　　*n.* 传记；传记作品
　　poetry ['pəʊətrɪ]　　*n.* 诗歌；诗集
◆blur [blɜ:(r)]　　*v.*（使）变得模糊不清；看不清
　　　　　　　　　　n.（移动的）模糊形状；模糊的记忆
◆flatter ['flætə(r)]　　*v.* 恭维；奉承；讨好（某人）
　　prejudice ['prejudɪs]　　*n.* 偏见；成见
◆banish ['bænɪʃ]　　*v.* 放逐；流放；把（某人）驱逐出境
◆preconception [,pri:kən'sepʃn]　　*n.* 预想；成见；事先形成的观念
★admirable ['ædmərəbl]　　*a.* 令人钦佩的；令人羡慕的；极好的
◆dictate [dɪk'teɪt]　　*v.* 口授；强行规定；摆布；指使
◆accomplice [ə'kʌmplɪs]　　*n.* 同谋；帮凶；共犯
　　criticize ['krɪtɪsaɪz]　　*v.* 批评；批判；评论；评价
★hint [hɪnt]　　*n.* 暗示；示意；(pl.) 建议；提示

Unit Seven Literature

     v. 暗示

◆imperceptible [ˌɪmpəˈseptəbl] *a.* 无法察觉的；感觉不到的

★twist [twɪst] *v.* 使扭曲；扭曲变形

     n. 转动；扭动

 steep [sti:p] *a.* 陡峭的；陡直的

     v. 深深浸泡；饱含（某品质）

◆acquaint [əˈkweɪnt] *v.* 使熟悉；使了解

 attempt [əˈtempt] *n.* 企图；试图

     v. 尝试；试图

 definite [ˈdefɪnət] *a.* 明确的；确切的；肯定的

 chapter [ˈtʃæptə(r)] *n.* 章；回；篇

◆impalpable [ɪmˈpælpəbl] *a.* 感触不到的；摸不到的；难解的

 element [ˈelɪmənt] *n.* 成分；要素；元素

★distinct [dɪˈstɪŋkt] *a.* 截然不同的；清楚的；明显的

★tone [təʊn] *n.* 腔调；语气；风气；气氛

◆comic [ˈkɒmɪk] *a.* 使人发笑的；可笑的；滑稽的

◆tragic [ˈtrædʒɪk] *a.* 可悲的；悲痛的

 contain [kənˈteɪn] *v.* 包含；容纳

Phrases and Expressions

 separate from 与……分离

◆hang back 退缩不前

 prevent from 防止

Proper Names

Virginia Woolf 维吉尼亚·伍尔夫（英国小说家）

Read and Choose

V. There are five questions or unfinished statements in the following. For each of them there are four choices marked A, B, C and D. Decide the best answer according to Passage Two.

1. What can books be classified into according to the passage?

  A) Books can be classified into fiction, biography, and poetry.

B) Books can be classified into novel, poetry, and fiction.

C) Books can be classified into novel, prose, and biography.

D) Books can be classified into fiction, prose, and biography.

2. Which of the following statements is NOT true according to the passage?

A) Most of the readers come to books with prejudice.

B) A reader often thinks the fiction shall be true, biography shall be flattering.

C) The author thinks we should banish all preconceptions when we read.

D) The author completely accepts the readers' opinion.

3. What should a reader do when he is reading?

A) The reader should banish all preconceptions.

B) Do not dictate to your author; try to become him.

C) Be writer's fellow-worker and accomplice.

D) All above.

4. What's the meaning of the underlined word in the sentence "Be his fellow-worker and accomplice."?

A) accomplish   B) accompany   C) confederate   D) corporation

5. What can we learn from the passage?

A) When reading you don't have to open your mind as widely as possible.

B) Even if steep yourself in reading, you won't find that your author is attempting to give you something definite.

C) Before reading we should think about how to read it.

D) Reading is good for job hunting.

VI. In this part, there are five sentences (the first four are taken from the two passages). Below each, there are five Chinese translations marked A, B, C, D and E. You should decide which the best translation is.

1. **We should live each day with gentleness, vigor and a keenness of appreciation which are often lost when time stretches before us in the constant panorama of more days and months and years to come.** *(Passage One)*

A) 我们一定会在每一天中都举止优雅、精力充沛、心怀感激，而所有这些，都是我们平日生活中容易忘却和丧失的，因为我们总以为自己将来还有很多的日子。

B) 我们一定会在每一天中都举止优雅、精力充沛、心怀感激，而所有这些，都是我们平日生活中容易忘却和丧失的，因为我们总以为在自己未来前面将有无尽的岁月和时日在延伸。

C) 我们每一天都要优雅地生活、有足够的体力并心怀感激，而所有这些，都是我们平日生活中容易忘却和丧失的，因为我们总以为在自己未来前面将有无尽的岁月和时日在延伸。

D) 我们常常忘记每天应该举止优雅、精力充沛、心怀感激，因为我们总以为在自己未来前面将有无尽的岁月和时日在延伸。

E) 我们应该每天都温柔地对待别人，精力要旺盛，要懂得欣赏，但是我们却经常忘记，因为还有很多的时间会来到。

2. **I have often thought it would be a blessing if each human being was stricken blind and deaf for a few days at some time during his early adult life.** *(Passage One)*

   A) 我常常想，如果每个人在他年轻时都能有几天突然失聪和失明，未尝不是一件幸事。
   B) 我常常想，如果每个人在他年轻时都能有几天突然失聪和失明，那并不是一件幸事。
   C) 我常常想，如果每个人在他成年初期都能有几天突然失聪和失明，未尝不是一件幸事。
   D) 我常常想，如果每个人在他成年初期忽然有几天看不见也听不见，未尝不是一件幸事。
   E) 我常常想，如果每个人在他成年初期忽然有几天看不见也听不见，那真是不幸。

3. **If we could banish all such preconceptions when we read, that would be an admirable beginning.** *(Passage Two)*

   A) 如果在我们阅读的时候能抛弃先入为主的观点，那么会有一个令人羡慕的开端。
   B) 当我们阅读的时候要摒弃个人观点，那么便会有一个好的开端。
   C) 如果我们能抛弃这样的观点，当我们阅读的时候就会令人羡慕的。
   D) 如果我们读书时什么也不想，那样开始以后就会引来很多人的羡慕的。
   E) 如果我们读书时能抛弃所有这些成见，那将是一个极可贵的开端。

4. **If you hang back, and reserve and criticize at first, you are preventing yourself from getting the fullest possible value from what you read.** *(Passage Two)*

   A) 如果你预约了以后又后悔了，就可以从开始的时候挑剔或批评阻止了你自己可能理解的书的价值。
   B) 假如你退缩不前，有所保留并且一开始就批评指责，你就在妨碍自己从你所读的书中得到最大的益处。
   C) 如果你一味退缩，有所保留又很挑剔的话，在开始的时候你就在妨碍自己从你所读的书中得到最大的益处。
   D) 如果你退缩不前，只知道批评指责，那么你就在阻止你自己完全理解你开始的时候所能读的书的价值。
   E) 如果你不前进，一开始就有所保留地进行批评的话，那么你就在妨碍别人从所读的书中获得最大的价值。

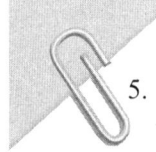

5. **English has replaced French in the world of diplomacy and German in the world of science.**

   A) 英语在外交方面替代了法语，在科学方面替代了德语。

   B) 在科学地与世界进行外交方面，英语代替了法语和德语。

   C) 在外交世界里英语替代了法语，在科技世界英语代替德语。

   D) 英语在法国作为外交用语，然而在德国却成了科技用语。

   E) 英语在外交方面取代了法语的地位，如同科技取代了德语。

Section III Grammar

Inversion（倒装）

倒装（inversion）是一种语法手段，用以表示一定句子结构的需要或强调某一句子成分的需要。英语的最基本的结构是主、谓结构，倒装就是将这种比较固定的次序加以颠倒。

倒装有两种。将主语和谓语完全颠倒过来，叫做完全倒装（complete inversion）。只将助动词（包括情态动词）移至主语之前，叫做部分倒装（partial inversion）。

Review and Practice

VII. There are 10 incomplete sentences below. For each one, there are four choices marked A, B, C and D. You should choose the best answer.

1. Only when you realize the importance of foreign languages _____ them well.

   A) you can learn   B) can you learn

   C) you learned   D) did you learn

2. Here _____!

   A) the train comes   B) comes the train

   C) coming the train   D) come the train

3. Not only _____ to stay at home, but he was also forbidden to meet his family.

   A) he was forcing   B) he was forced

   C) was he forcing   D) was he forced

4. So small _____ that I could hardly see it.

   A) be the school   B) the school was

   C) the school been   D) was the school

5. _____ at your lessons, you would have passed the exam.
   A) Have you worked hard   B) You had worked hard
   C) You have worked hard   D) Had you worked hard
6. Under the table _____ a lovely cat.
   A) lying was   B) lying were
   C) was lying   D) were lying
7. In this chapter _____ .
   A) will be found a picture   B) a picture will be found
   C) find a picture   D) a picture be found
8. Hardly_____ down _____ my son came in to ask me for some money.
   A) had I sat; than   B) I had sat; when
   C) had I sat; then   D) had I sat; when
9. No sooner _____ asleep than she heard a violent knock at the door.
   A) she had fallen   B) had she fallen
   C) she had fell   D) had she fell
10. His brother has not seen much of him recently._____ his parents.
    A) Neither did   B) So did
    C) Neither has   D) So hasn't

VIII. Correct the errors in the following sentences.

1. In a girl came with a bunch of flowers in her hand.
2. Never I have found him in such a good mood.
3. Only yesterday he found out that his watch was missing.
4. Not only he complained about the food, he also refused to pay for it.

Section IV   Writing

Business Letter（商务信函）

A business letter is the principal means used by a business firm to keep in touch with its customers; often enough it is the only one and customers form their impressions of the firm from the tone and quality of the letters it sends out. Business does not call for the elegant language of the poet, but it does require us to express ourselves accurately in plain language. So the secret of a good business letter is to write simply, in an easy and natural way—like one friendly human being talking to another. In other words, try to make your letters sound as much as possible like good conversations.

Sample

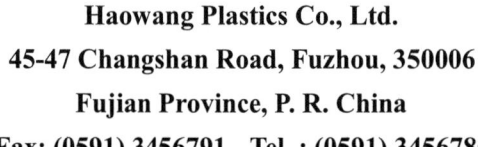

Haowang Plastics Co., Ltd.
45-47 Changshan Road, Fuzhou, 350006
Fujian Province, P. R. China
Fax: (0591) 3456791   Tel. : (0591) 3456786

9 Jan. , 2015

Thomson Plastics Co., Ltd.
567 Causeway Bay
Hong Kong

Dear Sir or Madam,

We learn from the Web that you are a leading manufacturer and sales agent of plastic products in Hong Kong. We are very much interested in importing plastic toys from Hong Kong. We should be obliged if you will let us have detailed information about the toy range you produce.

Please indicate any new items not yet introduced in China and send some samples if possible.

We await your early reply. Thank you.

Yours faithfully,
Alex Cheng
Manager of Imp/Exp Department

IX. Write a business letter.

远洋有限公司
约翰街8号
伦敦
电话号码：（01902）322479
传真号：（01902）322739
电子邮件：li1968@wlv.ac.uk

尊敬的先生/小姐，

在上述地址，我们想请贵公司参加于四月二十九日到五月四日举办的 2015 国际商品交易会，关于交易会的详情我们一周内将寄给您。

希望不久能收到您的来信，并能来参加。

李建林
敬上

Section V Enjoy Yourselves

A Red, Red Rose

——by Robert Burns

O, my luve's like a red, red rose,
That's newly sprung in June;
O, my luve's like the melodie,
That's sweetly played in tune.

As fair art thou, my bonnie lass,
So deep in luve am I;
And I will luve thee still, my dear,
Till a' the seas gang dry.

Till a' the seas gang dry, my dear,
And the rocks melt wi' the sun;
And I will luve thee still , my dear,
While the sands o' life shall run.

And fare thee weel, my only luve,
And fare thee weel a while!
And I will come again, my luve,
Tho' it were ten thousand mile!

Unit Eight News

➢ Warm-up Question

What's news? What kind of news do you like best?

Section I   Listening & Speaking

◆ Listening

Task 1.

Directions: In this section, you will hear 6 short conversations. At the end of each conversation, a question will be asked about what was said. Both the conversation and the question will be spoken twice. After each question there will be a pause. During the pause you must read the four choices marked A), B), C) and D), and decide which is the best answer. Then mark your answer.

Example:

You will hear:

M: Is it possible for you to work late, Miss Green?

W: Work late? I suppose so, if you really think it's necessary.

Q: Where does the conversation most probably take place?

You will read:

A) At the office.

B) In the waiting room.

C) At the airport.

D) In a restaurant.

From the conversation we know that the two were talking about some work they had to finish in the evening. This is most likely to have taken place at the office. Therefore, A) "At the office" is

Unit Eight News

the best answer. You should choose answer A).

Sample Answer

A)   B)   C)   D)

Now let us listen to 6 short conversations, both the conversation and the question will be spoken twice.

1. A) 15 words a minute.   B) 45 words a minute.
    C) 80 words a minute.   D) 18 words a minute
2. A) Sports.   B) History.
    C) News.   D) Discovery
3. A) French.   B) Spanish.
    C) Japanese.   D) English.
4.

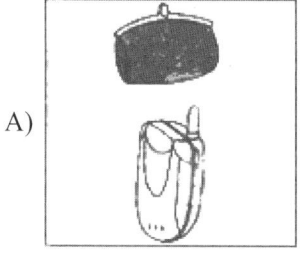 

A)   B)

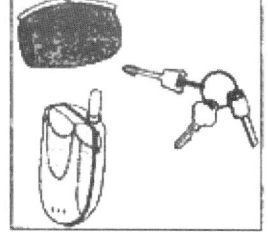 

C)   D)

5. A) In a classroom.   B) In a library.
    C) In a bookstore.   D) In a restaurant
6. A) ￡7.5.   B) ￡15.
    C) ￡50.   D) ￡30.

Task 2.

Directions: In this section, you will hear a short passage. At the end of the passage, you will

hear two questions. Both the passage and the questions will be spoken twice. After you hear one question, you must choose the best answer from the four choices marked A), B), C) and D). Then mark your answer.

1. A）interests   B）attractions
   C）benefits   D）profits
2. A）The customer found something wrong with his account.
   B）There was a huge amount of information being downloaded.
   C）There was a wrong money transaction.
   D）The hacker proudly admitted his successful break-in.

Task 3.

Directions: In this section, you will hear a passage three times. Listen carefully during the first reading. Then listen to the passage again. When it is being read the second time, you should fill in the ten blanks numbered from S1) to S10) with the exact words or phrases you have just heard. Finally, when the passage is read for the third time, you should check what you have written.

Handbook of Independent Journalism

What is News?

The answer to the question "What is news?" may seem obvious. News is what is new; it's what's happening.

Look it up in the dictionary, and you'll find "news" is S1) _____ as "a report of recent events or S2) _____ unknown information." But most of the things that happen in the world every day don't find their way into the news paper or onto the air in a S3) _____.

So what makes a story news worthy enough to be S4) _____ or broadcast? The real answer is, it S5) _____ a variety of factors. Generally speaking, news is S6) _____ that is of broad interest to the intended audience, so what's big news in Buenos Aires may not be news at all in Baku. Journalists decide what news to cover based on many of the following "news values".

(Excerpted from the U.S. Department of State publication, *Handbook of Independent Journalism*.)

◆ **Speaking**

Task 1. Talk about some news attracting a lot of people around you.

Task 2. Two students are in a pair to make a conversation as the following samples.

Sample 1

—I'm so excited.

—What are you excited about?

—Have you heard the news?

—No, what happened?

—You got a raise.

—That's right, I got a raise, but that's not my news.

Sample 2

—Have you heard the news?

—No, what happened? What's the news you want to let us know?

—Actually, you already know the news.

—Peter has a new baby grand daughter. And I'll tell you the truth.

—It's so exciting.

—That's good news. /That's a good piece of news.

Section II   Passage One

Meet Disney Characters in Shanghai

Can't you wait for the opening of the Shanghai Disney Resort in 2015? Meet Mickey and Minnie

Mouse and all their friends at the city's largest Disney exhibition at the Shanghai Super Brand Mall.

The exhibition invites visitors to have a taste of the Disneyland under construction, according to the organizer. Many of the exhibits have been transported from the Walt Disney Family Museum in Los Angeles, like the manuscripts of early animation producers.

The center of the mall's third floor has been transformed into a magic house with a giant Mickey above, greeting visitors. Classic cartoon figures, created by the company and its sub-companies over the past 90 years, are presented, including Winnie the Pooh.

Visitors can enjoy one of Disney's earliest films, Steamboat Willie. The film, which was screened in New York City in 1928, was considered the first fully synchronized sound cartoon. It was also the first time that Mickey and Minnie appeared.

Visual and audio technologies have been applied to make the exhibition interactive.

In the Snow White section, a magic mirror on the wall will astonish visitors. Like the evil queen in the fairytale, visitors can stand before the mirror and ask: "Mirror, mirror, on the wall, who's the fairest of them all?" One can see images of Snow White appear in the mirror. Snow White and the Seven Dwarfs, produced by the company, were considered the world's first full-length animated featured film.

In the Lion King section, visitors can stand at a designated position and enjoy the songs from the film in surround sound. The Lion King, Disney's 32nd full-length animated film, was one of the most successful Disney films and was turned into a Broadway opera.

Still the most charming star of the exhibition is Mickey Mouse, while the brightest of all is a Mickey Mouse model inlaid with more than 20,000 Swarovski crystals.

Four young artists, Yan Wei and Guan Chun from the Chinese mainland, and Dorophy Tang and Kenny Wang from Hong Kong, created different series of Mickey Mouse models with their personal styles.

Besides Disneyland, in 2015, the Walt Disney Company China will open the world's largest Disney Store, which will cover about 5,000 sq. m in Lujiazui, Shanghai's financial hub.

(Words 372)

(Excerpted from http://www.chinadaily.com.cn/language_tips/news/2014-01/23/content_17253018.htm)

New Words (★三级词汇　◆超纲词汇)

resort [rɪˈzɔːt]　　v. 求助于或诉诸某事物
　　　　　　　　　n. 求助；娱乐场，度假胜地；采用的办法
exhibition [ˌeksɪˈbɪʃn]　n. 陈列，展览；展览品
transport [ˈtrænspɔːt]　v. 运送，运输
　　　　　　　　　　　n. 运输
◆manuscript [ˈmænjuskrɪpt]　n. 手稿；原稿；底稿
◆animation [ˌænɪˈmeɪʃn]　n. 生气，活泼；动画片制作
transform [trænsˈfɔːm]　v. 使变形，使转变；改造，改善，改革
◆synchronized [ˈsɪŋkrənaɪzd]　a. 同步的
★technology [tekˈnɒlədʒɪ]　n. 科技（总称）；工业技术；工艺学
◆fairytale [ˈfeərɪteɪl]　a. 童话式的，童话中才有的，优美无比的
◆designate [ˈdezɪgneɪt]　v. 指明；指派；意味着；把……定名为
　　　　　　　　　　　　a. 指定而尚未上任的；选出而尚未上任的
★crystal [ˈkrɪstl]　n. 水晶，石英晶体；晶体
　　　　　　　　　a. 水晶制的，晶体的

Phrases and Expressions

have a taste of　体会；领略
according to　根据，依据
apply to　适用于；运用；致力于；
turn into　（使）变成；译成；成为
a series of　一系列；一连串

Proper Names

Mickey and Minnie Mouse　米奇和米妮
Shanghai Super Brand Mall　上海正大广场
The Walt Disney Family Museum　华特迪士尼家族博物馆
Winnie the Pooh　维尼小熊
Steamboat Willie　威利号汽船
Snow White and the Seven Dwarfs　白雪公主和七个小矮人
Lion King　狮子王
Broadway opera　百老汇音乐剧

Swarovski 施华洛世奇
Dorophy Tang 邓卓越 香港青年女艺术家

Read and Think

I. Answer the following questions according to the passage.

1. When did Mickey and Minnie first appear?
2. Which film was considered the world's first full-length animated featured film?
3. What is the most charming star of the exhibition?

Read and Try

II. Fill in each blank with a right word in its right form using the words in the following box.

| transport | transform | consider | present |
| technology | designate | exhibition | resort |

1. The _____ gives local artists an opportunity to display their work.
2. The sofa can _____ for use as a bed.
3. Ken is not _____, so I shall accept the prize on his behalf.
4. We must _____ these matters as a whole.
5. I _____ you to act for me while I am away.
6. Computer _____ has come a long way since the 1970s.
7. In this _____ you can enjoy all the comfort and convenience of modern tourism.
8. It is easier to travel if you have your own _____.

III. There are eight incomplete sentences below. For each sentence, there are four choices marked A, B, C and D. You should choose the proper one to complete each sentence.

1. This is the place _____ we visited last year. It is very beautiful.
   A) where   B) which   C) in which   D) why

2. My computer _____ by an unknown virus.
   A) has attacked   B) have attacked
   C) had been attacked   D) has been attacked

3. The teacher demands that students should _____ their test papers within two hours.
   A) turn in   B) turn into   C) turn up   D) turn on

4. _____ the sports meet will be put off, so now I am not busy.
   A) I've been told B) I've told C) I'm told D) I told
5. A series of debates_____ to be held.
   A) scheduled B) are scheduled C) is scheduled D) schedules
6. This is the only one of the books _____ has been recommended.
   A) where B) which C) that D) who
7. We should ____what we have learnt _____ our practical work.
   A) apply for B) apply to C) apply at D) apply in
8. She is constantly _____and it is affecting her health.
   A) under pressure B) under construction
   C) under control D) under repair

Read and Translate

IV. Translate the following sentences into English.
1. 在不久的将来，中国人就可以方便地体会到美国文化了。（have a taste of ）
2. 据目击者说，飞机起飞后不久就爆炸了。（according to）
3. 这些原则适用于学习英语。（apply to）
4. 这个学生总是问他老师一连串的问题。（a series of）

Reading Skills

Understanding Characters

Characters are persons in short stories, plays and novels. Writers always make their characters think and act like real people by giving them personalities. Generally the characters establish relationships, create or resolve conflict and offer different points of view regarding the events within the story. Therefore, understanding the characters by analyzing them in the lines is one of the steps of comprehending the works.

Directions: Read the following paragraphs carefully, and then choose the best answer.

Passage One

Frank Smithson was overjoyed when he read the letter, "Bigwoods Football Pools would like to congratulate you. You have won half a million pounds." At 11:30 Frank arrived at work. "Please explain why you're so late," his boss said. "Go and jump in the lake," replied Frank, "I've just come into a little money so this is goodbye. Find someone else to shout at." That evening Frank was smoking a very expensive Havana cigar when a knock was heard on the door. He rushed to the door. Outside were two men, "Mr. Smithson", one of them said, "We're from Bigwoods Pools. I'm afraid there's been a terrible mistake…"

(Words 95)

1. On hearing "…there's been a terrible mistake…" Frank was most likely to be _____.

   A) disappointed   B) worried

   C) nervous   D) curious

   Passage Two

   If I'm able to build myself a house there, I'll take my mother to live with me. I'll divide the house in two and keep her there. That would be a good life, living in the country in Puerto Rico with my wife and with everything that I own here; my TV set, the record player, and all. And with the rest of my family near me. Everyday I wake up with that hope. Although I have doubts, too, now and then. Sometimes I have a dream. I see myself leaving New York and going back to Puerto Rico, but when I get there I find myself friendless and alone.

(Words 110)

2. This character is _____.

   A) a wanted man   B) a loner

   C) a drifter   D) a family man

   Passage Three

   Lucy repented losing her temper. "I shouldn't have talked that way to Jean when she suggested that the perspective in my painting wasn't quite right. But it seems I always feel that people are attacking me when they make suggestions, even helpful ones, about anything I do.

(Words 55)

3. I guess I just don't know how to _____.

   A) be nice to anyone   B) make friends

   C) take criticism   D) paint very well

   Passage Four

   When the headman returned he brought with him a small, stocky, heavily-muscled man whom he introduced as Jeepo. The headman explained that the name was not a native name. He was called Jeepo because of his reputation as a famous mechanic in the maintenance and repair of jeeps. Atkins didn't listen too closely to what the headman was saying. He was studying Jeepo and he liked what he saw. Jeepo looked like a craftsman. His fingernails were as dirty as Atkins', and his hands were also covered with dozens of little scars. Jeepo looked back steadily at Atkins without humility or apology, and Atkins felt that in the mechanic's world of bolts and nuts, pistons, and good black oil he and Jeepo would understand one another.

Unit Eight　News

(Words 126)

4. Jeepo's character is revealed especially through_____.
　A) his speech　　　　　　　　　B) his thoughts
　C) his appearance　　　　　　　D) the speech and thoughts of others

Section II　Passage Two

Migrants to Be Quizzed on English Skills before Benefits

　　Migrants to the UK are to be quizzed about their English skills before being able to claim income-related benefits, the government has announced.

　　In a move to "protect the integrity of the benefits system", people will also be asked what efforts they have made to find work before coming to Britain.

　　Work and Pensions Secretary Iain Duncan Smith said people should not be able to "take advantage" of British benefits. Job centres in England, Scotland and Wales will use the "more robust" test.

　　The Department for Work and Pensions (DWP) said the test would ensure "only migrants who have a legal right to be in Britain and plan to contribute to this country can make a claim for benefits".

　　"For the first time, migrants will be quizzed about what efforts they have made to find work before coming to the UK and whether their English language skills will be a barrier to them finding employment," the DWP said in a statement.

　　Income-related benefits include council tax benefit, housing benefit, income-based job-seeker's allowance and pension credit.

　　Mr. Duncan Smith said British people were "rightly concerned" that migrants should contribute to the economy and should not be "drawn here by the attractiveness of our benefits system". "It is vitally important that we have strict rules in place to protect the integrity of our benefits system," he said.

He said the new test would help create a fair system which provided for "genuine" workers and job-seekers but "does not allow people to come to our country and take advantage".

To claim the benefits, migrants will have to pass a "habitual residence test" including more than 100 extra questions compared to now.

This will be overseen by an "intelligent IT system" which will ensure questions are "tailored to each individual claimant".

Migrants will be allowed to claim benefits if they can prove they are legally allowed to be in Britain and are "habitually resident" the country.

As part of this they might be questioned about what measures they have taken to "establish" themselves in Britain and what ties they still have abroad.

"They will also have to provide more evidence that they are doing everything they can to find a job," the DWP said.

(Words 370)

(Excerpted from http://www.chinadaily.com.cn/language_tips/news/2014-01/23/content_17253190.htm)

New Words（★三级词汇　◆超纲词汇）

◆migrant ['maɪɡrənt]　*n.* 移居者；移民
◆integrity [ɪn'teɡrətɪ]　*n.* 正直，诚实；完整
◆robust [rəʊ'bʌst]　*a.* 精力充沛的；坚定的；粗野的
◆habitual [hə'bɪtʃuəl]　*a.* 习惯的；惯常的；习以为常的
　intelligent [ɪn'telɪdʒənt]　*a.* 聪明的；理解力强的；有智力的
◆claimant ['kleɪmənt]　*n.* 原告；(贸易) 索赔人；提出要求者
　pension ['penʃn]　*n.* 退休金，养老金

Phrases and Expressions

contribute to　促成；有助于
take advantage of　利用
compare to　把……比作
in place　在适当的位置；适当的；在工作

Proper Names

Iain Duncan Smith　伊恩·邓肯·史密斯

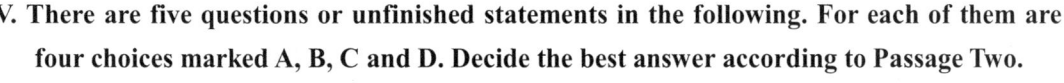

The Department for Work and Pensions (DWP) （英国）就业与退休保障部门，劳动和社会保障部门

Read and Choose

V. There are five questions or unfinished statements in the following. For each of them are four choices marked A, B, C and D. Decide the best answer according to Passage Two.

1. This passage mainly talks about _____.
   A) if you want to become a migrant to the UK, you should be quizzed about their English skills before being able to claim income-related benefits
   B) a quiz about English skills is to test whether their English is good or not
   C) income-related benefits
   D) an English test

2. What's the meaning of the word "barrier" in paragraph 5?
   A) fence   B) obstruction   C) difficulty   D) annoyance

3. Why will migrants also be asked what efforts they have made to find work before coming to Britain?
   A) Because the government wants to protect the integrity of the benefits system.
   B) Because the government wants to survey migrants.
   C) Because the government hates migrants.
   D) Because the government likes migrants.

4. What do not the income-related benefits include?
   A) Council tax benefit
   B) Housing benefit.
   C) Pension credit
   D) Scholarship

5. Which of the following statements is NOT the quiz to claim the benefits according to the passage?
   A) Passing a "habitual residence test".
   B) Proving they are legally allowed to be in Britain and are "habitually resident" the country.
   C) Providing more evidence that they are doing everything they can to find a job.
   D) Speaking English fluently.

VI. In this part, there are five sentences (the first four are taken from the two passages). For each sentence, there are five choices marked A, B, C, D and E. You are expected to make the best choice.

1. The film, which was screened in New York City in 1928, was considered the first fully synchronized sound cartoon. *(Passage One)*

    A. 这部电影是 1928 年上映的，纽约是世界上最早播出图片与声音同步的动画片的城市。
    B. 这部电影于 1928 年在纽约上映，堪称世界上最早的音像同步的动画片。
    C. 该影片于 1928 年在纽约上映，被认为是世界上第一部画面与声音同步的动画影片。
    D. 于 1928 年被纽约首播的影片，是世界上第一部图像与声音基本同步的动画影片。
    E. 该影片于 1928 年在纽约上映，是世界上第一部画面与声音完全同步的动画影片。

2. Visual and audio technologies have been applied to make the exhibition interactive. *(Passage One)*

    A. 展览采用了各种视听技术与游客进行互动。
    B. 各种视听技术已经被应用到展览互动过程中。
    C. 展览让游客应用了各种视听技术进行活动。
    D. 展览采用了各种视听技术让游客参加活动。
    E. 看和听的技术都已经被游客们用到了活动中。

3. "It is vitally important that we have strict rules in place to protect the integrity of our benefits system," he said. *(Passage Two)*

    A. 他说，"非常重要的一点就是我们要有严格的规定去保护福利制度。"
    B. 他说，"有严格的规章去保护福利制度的完善是至关重要的。"
    C. 他说，"设定严格的规则来确保福利制度的健全是至关重要的。"
    D. 他说，"在此处设定严格的规则去保护我们的福利很紧迫。"
    E. 他说，"我们设定严格的规则来确保福利制度的健全是很重要的。"

4. To claim the benefits, migrants will have to pass a "habitual residence test" including more than 100 extra questions compared to now. *(Passage Two)*

    A. 和现在相比，为了获得利益，移民将不得不进行 100 多道问题的常住居民测试。
    B. 与现在相比，为了领取救济金，移民还必须通过一份 100 多道问题的常住居民测试。
    C. 跟现在比较一下，为了领救济金，移民还必须通过一份 100 多道题的常住居民测试。
    D. 跟目前做比较，为了保持既得利益，100 多个移民将不得不通过常住居民测试。
    E. 为了认领到的利益，他们得通过 100 个移民问的常住居民测试方面的审查。

5. Working women have had more education than those who stay at home.

    A. 工作的妇女接受的教育要比那些待在家里的(妇女)接受的教育多。
    B. 工作的妇女拥有的教育要比那些待在家里的(妇女)拥有的教育多。

C. 正在工作的妇女们比呆在家里的(妇女们)更多。

D. 正在工作的妇女比那些呆在家里的(妇女)接受的教育多。

E. 正在工作的妇女比那些呆在家的妇女有更多的教育。

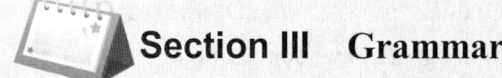

Agreement（一致）

　　一致（Agreement 或 Concord）是一个语法范畴，指组成句子的词之间在人称、单复数、所有格、词性等方面的一致。人称、所有格和词性的一致比较简单，单复数的一致涉及三个基本原则，即：

1. 语法一致（grammatical concord），即形式上的一致。
   主语为单数形式，谓语动词用单数形式；主语为复数形式，谓语动词也用复数形式。
   e.g.: The number of mistakes was surprising. 错误的数量很惊人。
2. 意义一致（notional concord），即意义或意念上的一致。
   1）主语形式虽为单数，但意义为复数，谓语动词要用复数形式。
   　　e.g.: My family are having supper now. 我们一家人现在正吃晚饭。
   2）主语形式为复数而意义上却是单数，谓语动词要用单数形式。
   　　e.g.: Thirty dollars is too expensive for this dictionary. 这本词典 30 美元太贵了。
3. 就近一致（principle of proximity），即谓语动词的单、复数形式取决于最靠近它的名词。
   e.g.: Not only the teacher but also his students like playing football.
   　　　不仅老师喜欢踢足球，而且学生也喜欢踢足球。

Review and Practice

VII. There are 10 incomplete sentences below. For each one, there are four choices marked A, B, C and D. You should choose the best answer.

1. Neither he nor I _____ for the plan.
   A) were　　　　　B) is　　　　　　C) are　　　　　　D) am
2. My father, together with his old friends _____ there already.
   A) will be　　　　B) had been　　　C) has been　　　 D) have been
3. Very few _____ her address in the city.
   A) has known　　 B) are knowing　　C) know　　　　　D) knows
4. Many a student _____ that mistake before.

    A) had made   B) has been made   C) have made   D) has made

5. No one but Jane _____ the secret. Nobody but Mary and I _____ in the classroom at that time.

    A) know; was   B) knows; was   C) know; were   D) knows; wcrc

6. The number of the people who _____ cars _____ increasing.

    A) own; are   B) own; is   C) owns; is   D) owns; are

7. It is not I but you who _____ the first to run to the goal in that competition.

    A) is   B) was   C) are   D) is going to

8. There _____ a pen, an ink bottle and some books on it. There _____ some bowls, plates and a spoon on it.

    A) is; are   B) are; are   C) are; is   D) is; is

9. What they have done _____ of great use to us. What he says and what he does _____ agree.

    A) is; not   B) is; do not   C) are; does not   D) are; not

10. When we are to hold the sports meeting _____ been decided. Whether succeeds or fails _____ matter.

    A) have; don't   B) has; don't   C) have; doesn't   D) has; doesn't

VIII. Fill in each blank with the appropriate word in the blackets.

1. Their earnings _____ (comes, come) to 1,000 dollars a week.
2. The United Nations _____ (was, were) formed in San Francisco in 1945.
3. _____ (Has, Have) skittles (九柱戏) been a popular game in England?
4. The football team _____ (is, are) being reorganized.
5. There _____ (was, were) nothing he could do and little he could say.

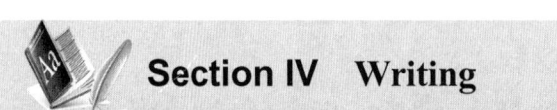

Section IV   Writing

News（新闻）

How to Write a News Story

Here's something very few people realise: Writing news stories isn't particularly difficult. It does take practice and not everyone will be an expert but if you follow the guidelines below you should be able to create effective news items without too much stress.

The Five "W"s and the "H"

This is the crux of all news—you need to know six things:

Who?   What?   Where?   When?   Why?   How?

Any good news story provides answers to each of these questions. You must drill these into your brain and they must become second nature.

For example, if you wish to cover a story about a local sports team entering a competition you will need to answer these questions:

Who is the team? Who is the coach? Who are the prominent players? Who are the supporters?

What sport do they play? What is the competition?

Where is the competition? Where is the team normally based?

When is the competition? How long have they been preparing? Are there any other important time factors?

Why are they entering this particular competition? If it's relevant, why does the team exist at all?

How are they going to enter the competition? Do they need to fundraise? How much training and preparation is required? What will they need to do to win?

The Inverted Pyramid

This refers to the style of journalism which places the most important facts at the beginning and works "down" from there. Ideally, the first paragraph should contain enough information to give the reader a good overview of the entire story. The rest of the article explains and expands on the beginning.

A good approach is to assume that the story might be cut off at any point due to space limitations. Does the story work if the editor only decides to include the first two paragraphs? If not, re-arrange it so that it does.

IX. **Try to write a news report by yourself.**

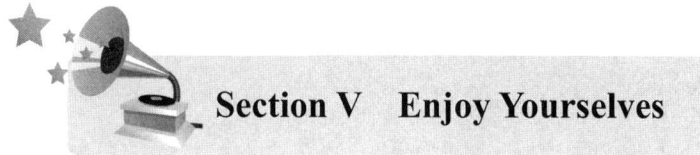

Section V   Enjoy Yourselves

Listen to the song.

Everytime

Notice me.
Take my hand.
Why are we strangers when?
Our love is strong.

Why carry on without me?
Everytime I try to fly
I fall without my wings.
I feel so small.
I guess I need you, baby.
And everytime I see you in my dreams.
I see your face, it's haunting me.
I guess I need you baby.
I make believe that you, are here.
It's the only way I see clear.
What have I done?
You seemed to move on easy.
Everytime I try to fly
I fall without my wings.
I feel so small.
I guess I need you baby.
And everytime I see you in my dreams.
I see your face.
You're haunting me.
I guess I need you, baby.
I may have made it rain.
Please forgive me.
My weakness caused you pain.
And this song is my sorry.
At night I pray
That soon your face will fade away
Everytime I try to fly
I fall without my wings.
I feel so small.
I guess I need you, baby.
And everytime I see you in my dreams.
I see your face.
You're haunting me.
I guess I need you, baby.

Appendix 1 Simulated Tests

Test One (Band Two)

Part I Listening Comprehension (15%)
Section A Short Conversations(10%)

Directions: *In this section, you will hear 10 short conversations. At the end of each conversation, a question will be asked about what was said. Both the conversation and the question will be spoken twice. After each question there will be a pause. During the pause, you must read the four choices marked A), B), C), D), and decide which is the best answer.*

1. A) She is leaving. B) She is reminding.
   C) She doesn't work today. D) She is running.
2. A) 11:00. B) 11:15. C) 11:45. D) 12:45.
3. A) 3:00. B) 3:30. C) 4:00. D) 4:30.
4. A) In a supermarket. B) At a hotel.
   C) In a pub. D) In a restaurant.
5. A) Duck, mushroom soup, seafood, chips.
   B) Mushroom soup, seafood, chips and coffee.
   C) Seafood, chips and dessert.
   D) Duck, seafood, chips and dessert.
6. A) The man. B) The woman.
   C) The man and the woman. D) The waiter.
7. A) Turn right. B) Go to the second crossing.
   C) Turn left. D) Go along the street.
8. A) The little boy. B) Delivery boy.
   C) The little girl. D) Serviceman.
9. A) Because he doesn't like it at all. B) Because he wants to save it.
   C) Because he has a toothache. D) Because he has a mouth problem.
10. A) Jack's son. B) The painter.

C) Jack himself. D) Someone else.

Section B A Short Passage (2%)

Directions: *In this section, you will hear a short passage. At the end of the passage, you will hear two questions. Both the passage and the questions will be spoken twice. After you hear one question, you must choose the best answer from the four choices marked A),B),C) and D).*

Questions 11 to 12 are based on the conversation you have just heard.

11. A) Anna Jarvis B) Julia Ward Howe
    C) Philadelphia D) Woodrow Wilson
12. A) On the fourth Sunday in June. B) On the second Sunday in May.
    C) On the second Sunday in June. D) On the second Sunday in March.

Section C Spot Dictation (3%)

Directions: *In this section, you will hear a passage three times. Listen carefully during the first reading, then listen to the passage again. When it is being read the second time, you should fill in the six blanks with the exact words or phrases you have just heard. Finally, when the passage is read for the third time, you should check what you have written.*

North Dakota is changing quickly because of the growth in the state's oil **S13)**_____. Money from oil has brought development and jobs. One unusual in North Dakota has been playing a part in this expansion. The bank of North Dakota **S14)**_____ in Bismark is the only state operated bank in the US. The bank's yearly report says it has had 10 straight years of record **S15)**_____. That includes years of the **S16)**_____ crisis of 2007 and 2008 when many banks failed. The bank provides or secures **S17)**_____ for local businesses. The bank of North Dakota was established in 1919, mainly to help control landing rate for farmers. Bank leader Eric White says the bank's purpose has changed over the years to support **S18)**_____ development. Mr. White has supervised part of that change and record growth.

S13)_____ S14)_____ S15)_____ S16)_____ S17)_____ S18)_____

Part II Structure and Vocabulary (35%)

Section A (15%)

Directions: *There are 15 incomplete sentences in this part. For each sentence, there are four choices marked A),B),C)and D). You must choose the one answer that best completes the sentence.*

19. Betty realized she_____.
    A) was making fun of B) is made fun of
    C) is being made fun of D) was being made fun of
20. If there were no examinations, we should have _____ in the college.
    A) a more happier time B) the happiest time
    C) much happiest time D) a much happier time
21. The tour group are waiting on _____ plane to take off.
    A) their B) his C) her D) its
22. _____ is good of you to help me to wash the clothes.
    A) That B) This C) It D) What
23. The way _____ you are doing it is completely wrong.
    A) on which B) of which
    C) at which D) in which
24. The teacher has his students_____ a diary every day.
    A) writing B) written C) to write D) write
25. When we got to the meeting-room, there were _____ left.
    A) only a few seats B) only few seats
    C) not a few seats D) a very few seats
26. I was ill that day, otherwise I _____ the sports meeting.
    A) took part in B) had taken part in
    C) would take part in D) would have taken part in
27. "At no time_____ in the meeting-room", said the manager.
    A) smoking is it permitted B) smoking is permitted
    C) does smoking permit D) is smoking permitted
28. Hardly ever_____ get a good interpersonal relationships these days without a good character.
    A) people can B) people might
    C) do people D) have people
29. Only recently _____ to deal with the sandstorm problems.
    A) something has done B) has something been done
    C) something has been done D) has something done
30. Many colleges can _____ dancing training courses to the students.
    A) pay B) offer C) manage D) receive
31. As I knew Mr.Hotter better, I discovered that my _____ had been right.

A) impression B) enjoyment C) environment D) improvement

32. It is much _____ to visit the website at *www. taobao.com*.

    A) fun B) happy C) interesting D) thing

33. I have _____ out of paper. Could you give me?

    A) spent B) run C) finished D) used

Section B (20%)

Directions: There are 20 incomplete sentences in this part. For each sentence, there are four choices marked A),B),C)and D). You must choose the one answer that best completes the sentence.

34. The manager must be very tired today; he doesn't seem to _____ on the discussion.

    A) concentrate B) put
    C) rely D) depend

35. It's necessary for the children to be a(n) _____ person.

    A) honest B) hopeful
    C) doubtful D) dishonest

36. Professor Lin is _____ his students' papers.

    A) correcting B) concluding
    C) coaching D) conducting

37. I enjoy listening to rock music, but my parents can't _____ it.

    A) sound B) stand
    C) want D) listen

38. What the boss said _____ like a huge amount of work.

    A) voices B) listens
    C) hears D) sounds

39. As soon as we finish the assignments, we'll start _____ for the concert in the evening.

    A) producing B) preparing
    C) preserving D) presenting

40. The teacher told him that success in school _____ much hard work.

    A) called for B) called on
    C) called back D) called at

41. He was really good at football, so his coach _____ him to take part in competitions.

    A) discouraged B) encouraged
    C) disclosed D) enclosed

42. Be sure to _____ the bike before you decide to buy it.

A) visit	B) inspire
C) look	D) inspect

43. The parents taught the little girl to _____ a knife and fork.
    A) take B) deal
    C) need D) handle

44. The boy couldn't open the box because the lid was too _____.
    A) thin B) tight
    C) loose D) thick

45. Betty was very glad because the Maths teacher _____ 90 to her.
    A) seized B) scolded
    C) scored D) screwed

46. My house _____ of five rooms—a living room, dining room, kitchen and two bedrooms.
    A) consists B) makes
    C) forms D) includes

47. I'm _____ cash at the moment. So I must go to the bank.
    A) short of B) few
    C) lack of D) sort

48. Keeping fit _____ to our good health.
    A) continues B) convinces
    C) contributes D) conveys

49. Read carefully and you will discover a(n) _____ meaning to the sentence.
    A) inner B) center
    C) outer D) middle

50. If you pay all your _____, you shall have no money to buy anything.
    A) decks B) debts
    C) details D) deeds

51. There are so many ladies in the _____.
    A) mail B) meal
    C) male D) mall

52. Some people are under heavy _____ of terrible working condition.
    A) prize B) reward
    C) rain D) pressure

53. In our spare time, we may also _____ ourselves in the pub.
    A) amuse B) arise

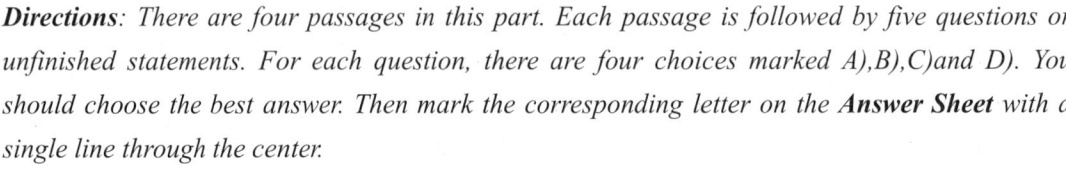

C) apply   D) amaze

Part III Reading Comprehension   (40%)

Directions: *There are four passages in this part. Each passage is followed by five questions or unfinished statements. For each question, there are four choices marked A),B),C)and D). You should choose the best answer. Then mark the corresponding letter on the **Answer Sheet** with a single line through the center.*

Passage One

　　There are many ways to find a job. It can be as easy as walking into a neighborhood store to look at its advertisement board. Local（本地的） stores often have areas where people can put small signs telling what kind of service they need or can provide. Such services include caring for children or cleaning houses.

　　Or, job searchers can look in the newspaper. Local newspapers have employment (招聘) advertisements placed by companies looking for workers.

　　Another popular tool for finding jobs is the Internet. For example, people in four hundred and fifty cities around the world can use the Craigslist (克雷格列表，网站名)site to buy objects, meet people or find a job. Craigslist says that it receives two million new job listings each month.

　　Another useful way to find a job is through a college or university. For example, students at the University of Texas in Austin can go to the Career Exploration Center to get help in finding a job. Of course, looking for a job requires knowing what kind of work you want to do. For example, there is a book called "What Color is Your Parachute (降落伞)?"by Richard Bolles. This book has been helping people to choose a job since it first came out in 1970.

　　Some experts also help people find jobs. Susan W. Miller owns a company called California Career Services in Los Angeles(洛杉矶). She says her company helps people to find jobs by first helping them understand their strengths, goals and interests. Then she provides them with methods and resources to help them to find the right job.

54. What is the passage mainly about?

　　A) Finding a job.   B) College students' part-time jobs.

　　C) Craigslist web site.   D) The relation between study and work.

55. By logging on the Craigslist web site, you can _____.

　　A) sell your old things   B) do some shopping online

　　C) create your own advertisement board   D) get useful information about 450 cities

56. "What Color is Your Parachute?" is a book which gives tips to those who want to _____.

A) work on the airplane B) buy a parachute
C) publish a book D) find a suitable job

57. It can be learned from the passage that _____.
   A) companies often put job information in local shops
   B) the Internet is the most popular tool for job hunters in the USA
   C) Susan W. Miller's company is helping people to choose careers
   D) California Career Services mainly serves for university students

58. How many ways of finding a job are mentioned in the passage?
   A) Three B) Four C) Five D) Six

Passage Two

Honesty may well be the policy, but it often deserts us when no one is watching, psychologists report today. Experiments with an honesty box to collect payments for hot drinks show that people are better at paying up when under the gaze of a pair of eyes. The surprise was that the eyes were not real, but photographed.

Researchers at Newcastle University set up the experiment in secret. They attached a poster to a cupboard of mugs above an honesty box alongside a kettle, with tea, coffee and milk. Over 10 weeks, they alternated each week between images of eyes and pictures of flowers.

Dr. Bateson, a behavioral biologist and leader of the study, said that even though the eyes were not real they still seemed to make people behave more honestly. The effect may arise from behavioral characteristics that developed as early humans formed social groups that increased their chances of survival. Individuals had to co-operate for the good of the group, rather than act selfishly.

"If nobody is watching us it is in our interests to behave selfishly. But when we think we're being watched we should behave better, so people see us as co-operative and behave the same way towards us," Dr. Bateson said.

"We thought we'd get a slight effect with eyes, by it was quite striking how much difference they made. Even at a subconscious level, it seems people respond to eyes, and that might be because eyes send a strong biological signal we have evolved(进化) to respond to."

The finding, which researchers believe <u>sheds light on</u> our evolutionary past, could be turned to practical use. The psychologists say images of eyes could promote ticket sales on public transport and improve monitor systems to prevent antisocial behavior.

59. This passage is mainly about _____.
   A) the policy of honesty B) an honesty box to collect money

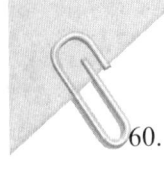

C) evolution on honesty D) an experiment on honesty

60. The reason for doing the experiment secretly is that the researchers _____.

    A) wanted to get a comparatively more exact result

    B) had known they wanted to do something illegally

    C) meant to get the co-operation of their colleagues

    D) intended to sell the hot drinks at a higher price

61. People behave honestly under watchful gaze of eyes because _____.

    A) they want to leave a good impression

    B) they fear to be laughed at by others

    C) they've got the nature through evolution

    D) they take the photo for a real pair of eyes

62. The underlined phrase "sheds light on" in the last paragraph means _____.

    A) causes somebody to become cheerful

    B) makes something easier to understand

    C) comes upon something by accident

    D) brings something into the broad daylight

63. Images of a pair of eyes can be applied to all except _____.

    A) ticket sales on public transport

    B) cold drink sales in public places

    C) places with "No spitting!" signs

    D) Christmas decorations in one's home

Passage Three

Walking across the campus of Pittsburgh's Carnegie Mellon University one delightful spring day, I came upon a table filled with young people chatting and enjoying the fine weather. Several had identical blue T-Shirts with "Trilogy@ CMU" written across them——Trilogy being an Austin, Texas-based software company with a reputation for recruiting(招聘) our top students. I walked over to the table. "Are you guys here to recruit?" I asked. "No, absolutely not," they replied firmly. "We're not recruiters. We're just hanging out, playing a little Frisbee(飞盘) with our friends." How interesting, I thought. They've come to campus on a workday, all the way from Austin, just to hang out with some new friends.

As I later learned, they were gifted students who had <u>inked</u> the highest-paying deal in the history of their department.

I asked one young man why he was going to a smaller city in Texas. The company is

excellent, he told me. There are also terrific people and the work is challenging. Though he had several good job offers from Pittsburgh's high-tech firms and knew the city well, he said he felt the city lacked the lifestyle options, cultural diversity, and tolerant attitude that would make it attractive to him. As he summed it up: "How would I fit in here?"

What a change from my own college days, just a little more than 20 years ago, when students would put on their dressiest clothes and carefully hide any counterculture tendencies to prove that they could fit in with the company. Today, apparently, it's the company trying to fit in with the students.

These young men and their lifestyle represent a lively new force in the economy and life of America. They are members of what I call the creative class: a fast-growing, highly educated, and well-paid part of the workforce on whose efforts corporate profits and economic growth increasingly depends. They do not consciously think of themselves as a class. Yet they share a common belief that values creativity, individuality, difference, and advantage.

64. What would be the best title for the passage?

    A) The rise of the creative class.

    B) New ideas about recruitment.

    C) Changed working cultures.

    D) A tale of two cities.

65. Why were the young people on the university campus?

    A) To get recruited in Pittsburgh.

    B) To celebrate their successful recruitment.

    C) To relax themselves away from work.

    D) To meet their old schoolmates.

66. The underlined word "inked" in paragraph 2 probably means "_____".

    A) fulfilled   B) obtained   C) settled   D) signed

67. Which of the following best describes the author's attitude towards the young people?

    A) Criticizing   B) Disappointing

    C) Approving   D) Disgusting

68. From the passage we can infer that _____.

    A) the young people prefer to work in a small quiet city

    B) the high pay is the main attraction to the young people

    C) Pittsburgh has many advantages over Austin

    D) Pittsburgh doesn't have enough attractions to the young people

Passage Four

CAMBRIDGE, Massachusetts (AP)—Bill Gates is finally getting his Harvard degree—32 years after he walked away from the university on the path to becoming the world's wealthiest person.

Gates, billionaire co-founder of Microsoft Corp, philanthropist (慈善家) and college dropout, will receive an honorary degree June 7 when he delivers Harvard University's 356th graduation address.

"His contributions to the world of business and technology, and the great example he has set through his far-reaching philanthropy, will rightfully put him on center stage in Harvard Yard," Harvard Alumni Association President Paul Finnegan said in a statement.

Gates is considered a member of Harvard's Class of 1977, which celebrates its 30th reunion this year. He first came to the university in 1973 but left in 1975 to devote his time to developing Microsoft, which he founded that year with childhood friend Paul Allen.

Gates helped turn Redmond, Wash—based Microsoft into the world's largest maker of computer software, with revenues of more than $44 billion during the year 2006. He was the company's chief executive(首席执行官)until 2000 and still serves as chairman.

Gates and his wife, Melinda, created the Bill and Melinda Gates Foundation in 2000, which is now the world's largest philanthropic foundation with an endowment(捐赠资金) of about $33 billion. The foundation concentrates on promoting global health, ending poverty and hunger, and <u>enhancing</u> education. The Gates Foundation also is a major donor to Harvard.

Jack Reardon, Harvard's associate vice president for university relations, said there was no particular reason why the university waited until this year to honor Gates. He said Harvard considers many people for honorary degrees every year.

Forbes magazine earlier this year estimated Gates' worth at $56 billion, making him the world's richest person.

69. Which of the following is probably the best title of this passage?

　　A) Bill Gates to become the world's richest person.

　　B) Bill Gates to give Harvard graduation address.

　　C) Bill Gates to create the largest philanthropic foundation.

　　D) Bill Gates to retire from Microsoft's chief executive.

70. Bill Gates will receive an honorary degree from Harvard because_____.

　　A) he is considered a member of Harvard's Class of 1977

　　B) he founded Microsoft and made it the world's largest maker of computer software

　　C) he is considering celebrating his 30th reunion in Harvard University this year

D) he has made great contributions to the world of business as well as philanthropy

71. The underlined word "enhancing" in the 6th paragraph probably means_____.

   A) enriching   B) improving
   C) moving   D) strengthening

72. Which of the following statements is NOT true?

   A) There have ever been 355 graduation addresses since.
   B) In 1975 Microsoft was founded by Gates and Paul Allen.
   C) Gates was one of the excellent graduates from Harvard.
   D) The Gates Foundation has donated a lot of money to Harvard.

73. We can conclude that Gates_____.

   A) will devote more of his energy to solving global problems
   B) would have been more successful with entire education in Harvard
   C) will not be willing to accept the honorary degrees from Harvard
   D) cares more about his reputation than anything else in the world

Part IV   Translation (10%)

Directions: *There are five sentences in this part. For each sentence, five suggested Chinese translations are given. There are five choices marked A,B,C, D and E. You are expected to make the best choice.*

74. Ben Franklin was by no means a cautious man.

   A) 富兰克林有时候是谨小慎微之人。
   B) 富兰克林绝不是谨小慎微之人。
   C) 富兰克林绝不是胆小慎微之人。
   D) 富兰克林不再是谨小慎微之人。
   E) 富兰克林不再是胆小慎微之人。

75. Where Are We Going, Dad? Presents a new generation of men who, in a break from Chinese tradition, now take an active role in their children's lives.

   A) 综艺节目《爸爸去哪儿》显示了新时代男人积极参与到子女生活中的情景。
   B) 综艺节目《爸爸去哪儿》显示了新时代男人打破中国传统，积极参与到子女生活中的情景。
   C) 综艺节目《爸爸去哪儿》展现了新时代男人，打破中国传统，积极参与到子女生活中的情景。
   D) 综艺节目《爸爸去哪儿》显示了新时代男人积极打破中国传统和子女生活的情景。

E) 综艺节目《爸爸去哪儿》展现了打破中国传统的新时代男人积极参与到子女生活中的情景。

76. The first thing you should do when you have a lot on your plate is to separate the tasks, just like the different squares of food in a meal.

A) 你应该做的第一项事情，当你有一堆事情等着处理的时候，是区分任务，就如同将食物分类一样。

B) 你应该做的第一项事情，当你有一堆食物等着处理的时候，是区分任务，就好像分类食物一样。

C) 当你有一堆食物等着处理的时候你应该做的第一项事情是区分任务，就如同将食物分类一样。

D) 当你有一堆事情等着处理的时候你应该做的第一项事情是区分任务，就如同将食物分类一样。

E) 当你有一堆事情等着处理的时候你应该做的第一项事情是区分任务，就好像分类食物一样。

77. For it turns out the most effective shopping sprees are the snappiest ones.

A) 研究证明，在购物狂潮中动作最快的人才是购物狂热的人。

B) 研究证明，在购物狂潮中动作最快的人才是喜欢购物的人。

C) 研究证明，在购物狂潮中动作最快的人才是购物狂。

D) 研究证明，在购物狂潮中动作最快的人才是购物的人。

E) 研究证明，在购物狂潮中动作最快的人才是最会买东西的人。

78. The Prince William will take a 10-week course in agricultural management, organized by the Cambridge University's Programme for Sustainability Leadership.

A) 威廉王子将参加一个 10 周农业管理课程，课程隶属于剑桥大学"可持续发展领导项目"。

B) 这个 10 周农业管理课程是为威廉王子量身定做的，是由剑桥大学"可持续发展领导项目"组织的。

C) 这个为威廉王子量身定做的 10 周农业管理课程是由剑桥大学"可持续发展领导项目"组织的。

D) 威廉王子将参加一个 10 周农业管理课程，课程隶属于"可持续发展领导项目"的剑桥大学项目。

E) 威廉王子将参加一个 10 周农业管理课程，课程由剑桥大学"可持续发展领导项目"组织。

Appendix 1　Simulated Tests

Test Two (Band Three)

Part I　Listening Comprehension　(15%)

Section A

Directions: *In this section, you will hear 10 short conversations. At the end of each conversation, a question will be asked about what was said. Both the conversation and the question will be spoken twice. After each question there will be a pause. During the pause you must read the four choices marked A), B), C), and D), and decide which is the best answer. Then mark the corresponding letter on the **Answer Sheet** with a single line through the center.*

Example:　You will hear:

　　　　　You will read:

　　　　　　　　　A) At the office.

　　　　　　　　　B) In the waiting room.

　　　　　　　　　C) At the airport.

　　　　　　　　　D) In a restaurant.

From the conversation we know that the two were talking about some work they had to finish in the evening. This is most likely to have taken place at the office. Therefore, A) "At the office" is the best answer. Therefore, you should choose answer A).

Sample Answer

~~A)~~　　B)　　C)　　D)

1. A) 5.　　　　　　　　B) 3.　　　　　　　　C) 8.　　　　　　　　D) 2.
2. A) He should take the test again.　　　　B) He should call to check his score.
　　C) He should get it from the computer.　　D) He should wait for some time.
3. A) 150.　　　　　　　B) 270.　　　　　　　C) 250.　　　　　　　D) 120.
4. A) To take a shopping card.　　　　　　B) To get a used card.
　　C) To go to the shop.　　　　　　　　　D) To get a new bank card.
5. A) In a department store.　　　　　　　B) In the woman's department.
　　C) In the toy department.　　　　　　　D) In a book store.
6. A) At 8:00 am.　　　　　　　　　　　　B) At 9:00 am.
　　C) At 8:30 am.　　　　　　　　　　　　D) At 7:30 am.
7. A) A healthy way of life.

B) An interesting book on Indians.

C) Whether they should move to America.

D) Whether they once lived in the same place.

8. A) He will buy some food.　　　　B) He will go to cinema.
   C) He will go shopping.　　　　　D) He will buy some books.
9. A) 10:00.　　　B) 9:00.　　　C) 9:30.　　　D) 10:30.
10. A) In a shop.　　　　　　　　　B) In a hotel.
    C) In a restaurant.　　　　　　　D) In a bank.

Section B

Directions: *In this section, you will hear a short passage. At the end of the passage, you will hear two questions. Both the passage and the questions will be spoken twice. After you hear one question, you must choose the best answer from the four choices marked A), B), C), and D). Then mark the corresponding letter on the* **Answer Sheet** *with a single line through the center.*

Questions 11 to 12 are based on the passage you have just heard.

11. A) They exercised less frequently.

    B) They had less sex.

    C) They were "uncomfortable" in their lives.

    D) They had poor nutrition.

12. A) fruit.　　　　　　　　　　B) meat.
    C) olive oil.　　　　　　　　　D) vegetables.

Section C　Spot Dictation

Dictions: *In this section, you will hear a passage three times. Listen carefully during the first reading. Then listen to the passage again. When it is being read the second time, you should fill in the six blanks numbered* **S1)** *to* **S6)** *with the exact words or phrases you have just heard. Finally, when the passage is read for the third time, you should check what you have written.*

A small village was troubled by a man-eating lion. So the leaders sent a **S1)**_____ to the great hunter, Jonesie, and asked him to come and kill the **S2)**_____. For several nights the hunter lay in wait for the lion, but it never appeared. Finally, he told the village chief to kill a cow and give him its hide. Draping the skin over his **S3)**_____, he went to the pasture to wait for the lion. In the middle of the night, the villagers woke to the sound of blood-curdling **S4)**_____ coming from the pasture. As they carefully **S5)**_____, they saw the hunter on the ground, groaning in pain. There was no **S6)**_____ of the lion. "What happened, Jonesie? Where is the lion?" asked the chief. "Forget the damn lion!" he howled. "Which one of you idiots let the bull loose?"

S1)_____ S2)_____ S3)_____ S4)_____ S5)_____ S6)_____

Part II Vocabulary and Structure (20%)

Directions: There are 20 incomplete sentences in this part. For each sentence there are four choices marked A), B), C), and D). You must choose the one answer that best completes the sentence.

13. The man said he _____ chapter one by the end of the month.
    A) would have covered B) would have cover
    C) will have covered D) should have covered

14. I met a lady _____ as an expert in history.
    A) known B) knowing
    C) to be known D) is known

15. Absolutely much attention _____ your math learning, because you are far behind.
    A) must pay to B) should be paid to
    C) would be paid to D) must be paid to

16. We know that the novel _____ 6 chapters.
    A) is consisted of B) consists of
    C) consists with D) be consisted with

17. There are eleven students _____ are always absent from meeting.
    A) whom B) who C) they D) them

18. It's suggested that the assignments _____ before class.
    A) will be done B) has to be done
    C) should have to be done D) be done

19. _____ Alice apologized to me, I won't forgive her.
    A) Because B) Even though
    C) Since D) Even that

20. _____ I met my uncle, I will speak my mind to him.
    A) Only if B) As if C) If only D) Even if

21. If I _____ you, I would pick up French in place of Japanese.
    A) were B) is C) be D) being

22. Not only _____ table tennis, but also takes interest in volleyball.
    A) does he like B) he likes C) he does like D) he liked

23. look! _____!
    A) There the train comes   B) There comes the train
    C) There does the train   D) There the train does come
24. _____, she is very good at playing table tennis.
    A) A girl as she is   B) A girl as is she
    C) Girl as she is   D) Girl as is she
25. _____ finish my housework when my telephone rang.
    A) Almost did I   B) Hardly did I
    C) Hardly I did   D) when I
26. Either his brother or his friends _____ his opinions .
    A) supporting   B) support
    C) supports   D) has supported
27. A large number of students_____ the lecture at present.
    A) is listening   B) listened
    C) are listening   D) were listening
28. One of the keys _____ a happy life is to have a good character and mood.
    A) live   B) to live   C) to living   D) have lived
29. What she said is not true, _____?
    A) is it   B) does it   C) do it   D) isn't it
30. Alice is the only one of the students who _____ from America.
    A) comes   B) come
    C) came   D) is coming
31. I never agree _____ my sister's opinion.
    A) for   B) with
    C) on   D) in
32. The monitor _____ the forms to the class for the teacher.
    A) presented   B) delivered
    C) distributed   D) handed in

Part III   Reading   Comprehension (40%)

Directions: *There are four passages in this part. Each passage is followed by five questions or unfinished statements. For each question, there are four choices marked A), B), C) and D). You should choose the best answer. Then mark the corresponding letter on the **Answer Sheet** with a single line through the center.*

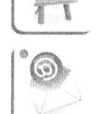

Passage One

Questions 39 to 43 are based on the following passage.

Room for Revolution: George Washington and His Philadelphia Friends.

March 16th, 2007-August 30 th, 2007, *Charles Willson Peal's George Washington at Princeton* is on view at the museum which was lent from a private collection. This visually striking and finely made life-size portrait（肖像）records Washington's 6-foot-2-inch figure in a pose highlighting strength, composure, and elegance. It is put up in a room neighboring to the Powel House parlor, a period room from one of Philadelphia's greatest eighteenth-century private homes, where Washington was frequently entertained by his friends, Samuel and Elizabeth Powel. Both spaces contain important examples of furniture by Philadelphia's finest craftsmen, such as Thomas Affect and John Aitken. Among these is a side chair specially ordered by the Washington when living in Philadelphia.

Painted in Philadelphia in 1779, Peale's painting was immediately sent to Europe to promote Washington's reputation as a leader and the cause of the American Revolution, then in progress. Later, during Europe's Napoleonic Wars, a Spanish duke with strong sympathies with American Revolution owned the picture. At that time he added the complicated carved caption to it, which described Washington as "a liberator of his country who abandoned absolute power."

Curators:

American Art Department Staff , website commentary by Carol Soltis

Location:

Galleries 286 and 287, second floor

33. This passage is mainly about _____.

　　A) the cause of American Revolution

　　B) the information of a portrait on view

　　C) the description of the life of George Washington

　　D) the friendship between Washington and his friends

34. What is the name of the portrait?

　　A) Room for Revolution.

　　B) Charles Wilson Peal.

　　C) George Washington at Princeton.

　　D) George Washington and His Philadelphia Friends.

35. What happened in the Powel House parlor?

　　A) Washington entertained his friends.

B) Washington made a chair on his own.

C) Charles Wilson Peal finished the portrait

D) Samuel and Elizabeth Powel met Washington a lot.

36. According to the passage, Washington _____.

A) lived between 1741 and 1827

B) ordered the portrait painted in 1779

C) was sympathized by a Spanish duke

D) was a great man not greedy for power

37. The passage tells us that _____.

A) when the portrait was finished, America was at war

B) the portrait was originally hanging in Samuel's room

C) the portrait was sent to Europe to gain support from Napoleon

D) the caption of the portrait was carved by Philadelphia's finest craftsmen

Passage Two

Questions 38 to 42 are based on the following passage

The people who built Stonehenge in southern England thousands of years ago had wild parties, eating barbecued pigs and breaking pottery. This is according to recent work by archaeologists—history experts who investigate how human beings lived in the past.

Archaeologists digging near Stonehenge last year discovered the remains of a large prehistoric village where they think the builders of the mysterious stone circle used to live. The village is about 4,600 years old, the same age as Stonehenge and as old as the pyramids in Egypt. It is less than two miles from the famous ancient landmark and lies inside a massive man-made circular dirt wall, or "henge", known as the Durrington Walls.

Remains found at the site included jewellery, stone arrowheads, tools made of deer antlers, wooden spears and huge amounts of animal bones and broken pottery. "These finds suggest Stone Age people went to the village at special times of the year to feast and party", says Mike Parker-Pearson from Sheffield University in England.

He said many of the pig bones they found had been thrown away half-eaten. He also said the partygoers appeared to have shot some of the farm pigs with arrows, possibly as a kind of sport before barbecuing them.

An ancient road which led from the village to the River Avon was also found. Here, the experts think, people came after their parties to throw dead relatives in the water so the bodies would be washed downstream to Stonehenge.

Parker-Pearson believes Stonehenge was like a cemetery where ancient Britons buried the dead and remembered their ancestors. "The theory is that Stonehenge is a kind of spirit home to the ancestors."

The recent discovery of the village within the Durrington Walls shows that Stonehenge didn't stand alone but was part of a much bigger religious site, according to Parker-Pearson.

People still come to worship and celebrate at Stonehenge today. They meet there when the sun sets on the shortest day of winter and when it rises on the longest day of summer. But the days of barbecuing whole pigs there and throwing family members into the river are a thing of the past.

38. What was Stonehenge according to the text?

A) A village where hundreds of people once lived.

B) A place that regularly hosted large parties.

C) A church where local villagers would get married.

D) A site where dead people were placed or remembered.

39. The underlined word "It" (paragraph 2) refers to _____.

A) the village   B) Stonehenge

C) the pyramid   D) the dirt wall

40. From the text, we can infer that the people who came to the village_____.

A) liked to drink wine   B) knew how to hunt

C) were from Egypt   D) lived by the River Avon

41. What do experts think people did after the village parties?

A) Returned to live at Stonehenge.

B) Prayed for good luck in the new year.

C) Hunted farm pigs as a sport.

D) Put their dead relatives in the river.

42. When do people most often go to Stonehenge today?

A) When a new discovery is made.

B) At the beginning of summer and winter.

C) On the longest and shortest days of the year.

D) When they want to have a barbecue.

Passage Three

Questions 43 to 47 are based on the following passage.

In cities with rent control, the city government sets the maximum rent that a landlord (房东) can charge for an apartment. Supporters of rent control argue that it protects people who are living in apartment. Their rent cannot increase; therefore, they are not in danger of losing their homes. However, the critics say that after a long time, rent control may have negative effects. Landlords know that they cannot increase their profits. Therefore, they invest in other businesses where they can increase their profits. They do not invest in new buildings which would also be rent-controlled. As a result, new apartments are not built. Many people who need apartments cannot find any. According to the critics, the end result of rent control is a shortage of apartments in the city.

Some experts argue that the minimum wage law can cause problems in the same way. The federal government sets the minimum that an employer must pay workers. The minimum helps people who generally look for unskilled, low-paying jobs. However, if the minimum is high, employers may hire fewer workers. They will replace workers with machinery. Therefore, other things being equal, the number of workers that employers want decreases. Thus, critics hold the opinion that an increase in the minimum wage may cause unemployment. Some poor people may find themselves without jobs instead of with jobs at the minimum wage.

Supporters of the minimum wage say that it helps people keep their dignity. Because of the law, workers cannot sell their services for less than the minimum. Furthermore, employers cannot force workers to accept jobs at unfair wages.

Economic theory predicts the results of economic decision, such as decisions about farm production, rent control, and the minimum wage. The predictions may be corrected only if "other things are equal". Economists do not agree on some of the predictions. They also do not agree on the value of different decisions. Some economists support a particular decision while others criticize it. Economists do agree, however, that there are no simple answers to economic questions.

43. There is the possibility that setting maximum rent may_____.

    A) cause a shortage of apartments

    B) worry those who rent apartments as homes

    C) increase the profits of landlords

    D) encourage landlords to invest in building apartments

44. We can safely say that rent control_____.

    A) will always benefit those who rent apartments

    B) is unnecessary

    C) will probably bring inactive effects in the long run

    D) is necessary under all conditions

45. There will be the problem of unemployment if_____.

    A) the minimum wage is set too high

B) the minimum wage is set too early

C) the workers are unskilled

D) the maximum wage is set for poor workers

46. The passage tells us about _____.

    A) the relationship between supply and demand

    B) the possible results of government controls

    C) the necessity of government control

    D) the urgency of getting rid of government control

47. Which of the following statements is NOT true?

    A) The results of economic decisions cannot always be predicted.

    B) Minimum wage cannot always protect employees.

    C) Economic theory can help predict the results of economic decision if other factors are not changing.

    D) Economists usually have the same prediction about an economic decision.

Passage Four

Questions 48 to 52 are based on the following passage

The old man walked with a cane(拐杖) slowly into the restaurant. His poor jacket, patched (打补丁的) trousers, and worn-out shoes made him stand out from the usual Saturday morning breakfast crowd. Unforgettable were his pale blue eyes that were bright like diamonds, large rosy cheeks, and thin lips held in a smile.

He walked toward a table by the window. A young waitress watched him and ran over to him, saying, "Here, Sir. Let me give you a hand with that chair." Without a word, he smiled and nodded a thank you. She pulled the chair away from the table. Steadying(稳住) him with one arm, she helped him move in front of the chair, and get comfortably seated. Then she pushed the table up close to him, and leaned his cane against the table where he could reach it.

In a soft, clear voice he said, "Thank you, Miss."

"You are welcome, Sir." She replied. "My name is Mary. I'll be back in a moment. If you need anything, just wave at me!"

After he had finished a hearty meal of pancakes, bacon, and hot lemon tea, Mary brought him the change, helping him up from his chair and out from behind the table. She handed him his cane, and walked with him to the front door. Holding the door open for him, she said, "Come back and see us, Sir!"

He nodded a thank you and said softly with a smile, "You are very kind!"

When Mary went to clean his table, she was surprised. Under his plate she found a business card and a note written on the napkin, under which was a $100 bill. The note on the napkin read, "Dear Mary, I respect you very much, and you respect yourself, too. It shows by the way you treat others. You have found the secret of happiness. Your kind gestures will shine through those who meet you."

The man she had served was the owner of the restaurant. This was the first time that she, or any of his employees, had seen him in person(亲自).

48. The relationship between the old man and Mary was _____.
    A) father and daughter   B) employer and employee
    C) waiter and customer   D) uncle and nephew

49. Based on the passage, all of the following words can be used to describe Mary except _____.
    A) kind   B) considerate   C) helpful   D) calm

50. Mary ran over to the old man because _____.
    A) the old man was the boss of the restaurant
    B) she saw the old man had some difficulty moving and taking a seat
    C) she was worried that the old man might cause trouble to the restaurant
    D) the old man had asked her to wait on him

51. The man came to the restaurant _____.
    A) to have breakfast
    B) to see his employees
    C) to find out how his restaurant was working
    D) to see how Mary served customers

52. The words the man left on the napkin indicated that _____.
    A) respecting others means respecting oneself
    B) serving others is a respectable job
    C) Mary would get a rise as a result of her kindness
    D) Mary's kind service would bring in more money for her

Part IV   Translation from English into Chinese   (10%)

Directions: *There are five sentences in this part. For each sentence, five suggested Chinese translations are given. There are five choices marked A, B, C, D and E. You are expected to make the best choice.*

T1. (line2-3, Para.1, Passage 2)

This is according to recent work by archaeologists—history experts who investigate how

human beings lived in the past.
- A) 这是考古学家得出的结论，他是研究古代人民如何生活的
- B) 这是依据考古学专家得出结论的近来的报告，他是研究古代人民如何生活的
- C) 这是依据研究古代人民生活的考古学专家的最新报告得出的结论。
- D) 这是依据研究古代人民生活的考古学专家的报告得出的结论。
- E) 这是依据考古学专家近来的报告得出的结论，他是研究古代人民如何生活的。

T2. (line2-3, Para.2, Passage 2)

The village is about 4,600 years old, the same age as Stonehenge and as old as the pyramids in Egypt.
- A) 这个村庄有大约 4,600 年的历史，和巨石阵一样大，埃及金字塔一样古老。
- B) 这个村庄有大约 4,600 年的历史，和巨石阵，埃及金字塔一样古老。
- C) 这个村庄有大约 4,600 年的历史，和巨石阵一样古老，埃及金字塔一样大。
- D) 这个村庄有大约 4,600 年的历史，巨石阵，埃及金字塔都没有它古老。
- E) 这个村庄有大约 4,600 年的历史，和巨石阵，埃及金字塔一样老。

T3. (line8, Para.1, Passage 3)

According to the critics, the end result of rent control is a shortage of apartments in the city.
- A) 根据批评家所言，这个城市租金管制的最终结果将是公寓的短缺。
- B) 根据批评家的话，这个城市租金管制的最终结论是公寓的短缺。
- C) 根据批评家的话，这个城市租金管制的最终结局是公寓的短缺。
- D) 根据批评家所言，租金管制的最终结果将是这个城市公寓的短缺。
- E) 根据批评家所言，租金管制的最终结果将导致这个城市公寓的短缺。

T4. (line1-2, Para.3, Passage 3)

Because of the law, workers cannot sell their services for less than the minimum.
- A) 因为法律，工人们不能以低于最低工资的标准出卖服务。
- B) 因为法律，工人们不能以最低工资的标准出卖劳动力。
- C) 因为法律，工人们不能以最低工资的标准出卖服务。
- D) 因为法律，最低工资标准使工人们无法随便出卖劳动力。
- E) 因为法律，工人们不能以低于最低工资的标准出卖劳动力。

T5. Many websites have carried this photo.
- A) 很多网站取消了这张照片。
- B) 很多网站下载了这张照片。
- C) 很多网站拦截了这张照片。
- D) 很多网站报道了这张照片。
- E) 很多网站登载了这张照片。

Part V Writing (15%)

Direction: *For this part you are allowed 30 minutes to write a composition of no less than 100 words on* **Low-carbon Life**. *Remember your composition must be written according to the following outline. Write your composition on the* ***Composition Sheet.***

Outline:

1. 现在人们过低碳生活的必要性。
2. 生活中怎么做才算是低碳生活。

Words for Reference:

low-carbon, emissions, dioxide, air pollution

Appendix 2

Words and Expressions

(★三级词汇　◆超纲词汇)

A

◆abolish [əˈbɒlɪʃ]　v. 废除；废止　　　　　　　　　　　　　　　　　　　U6a
　accomplice [əˈkʌmplɪs]　n. 同谋；帮凶；共犯　　　　　　　　　　　　U7b
★accomplish [əˈkʌmplɪʃ]　v. 完成，实现　　　　　　　　　　　　　　　U2b
◆acquaint [əˈkweɪnt]　v. 使熟悉；使了解　　　　　　　　　　　　　　　U7b
★additional [əˈdɪʃənl]　a. 外加的，附加的，额外的　　　　　　　　　　U2a
★admirable [ˈædmərəbl]　a. 令人钦佩的；令人羡慕的；极好的　　　　　U7b
★adopt [əˈdɒpt]　v. 收养；采用；正式通过；选定　　　　　　　　　　　U5a
　advanced [ədˈvɑːnst]　a. 高级的；先进的　　　　　　　　　　　　　　U6b
◆affection [əˈfekʃn]　n. 喜爱；钟爱　　　　　　　　　　　　　　　　　U1a
　affordable [əˈfɔːdəbl]　a. 付得起的；买得起的　　　　　　　　　　　U1b
　agriculture [ˈæɡrɪkʌltʃə(r)]　n. 农业　　　　　　　　　　　　　　　U6a
　alternative [ɔːlˈtɜːnətɪv]　a. 可用以代替其他事物的；另一可选用的；其他的
　　　　　　　　　　　　　　　n. 可能性中的选择；可能性之一　　　　U3a
★amend [əˈmend]　v. 修正；修订　　　　　　　　　　　　　　　　　　U6a
★amendment [əˈmendmənt]　n. 修正；修订　　　　　　　　　　　　　　U6a
　amount [əˈmaʊnt]　n.　(of sth) 总数；总额；总值；数量
　　　　　　　　　　　v.　(to sth) 总计；共达；等于或相当于某事物　　U3a
◆animation [ˌɪnɪˈmeɪʃn]　n. 生气，活泼；动画片制作　　　　　　　　　U8a
★anniversary [ˌænɪˈvɜːsəri]　n. 周年；周年纪念　　　　　　　　　　　U6a
　anxiety [æŋˈzaɪəti]　n. 焦虑；忧虑；害怕；渴望　　　　　　　　　　U4a
　application [ˌæplɪˈkeɪʃn]　n. 申请；请求；应用；运用　　　　　　　U5a
　appreciate [əˈpriːʃieɪt]　v. 感激，感谢，欣赏　　　　　　　　　　　U2a
　astonish [əˈstɒnɪʃ]　v. 使十分惊讶；使大为惊奇；使吃惊　　　　　　U4a

attempt [ə'tempt]   n. 企图；试图   U7b
attendant [ə'tendənt]   n. 服务员；侍者；随从；护理员
　　　　　　　　　　　a. 伴随的；随之而来的   U4a
available [ə'veɪləbl]   a. 可获得的；可购得的；可找到的   U3b
◆aviation [ˌeɪvɪ'eɪʃn]   n. 航空   U4a

B

◆banish ['bænɪʃ]   v. 放逐；流放；把（某人）驱逐出境   U7b
benefit ['benɪfɪt]   n. 利益；实惠；好处   U3a
◆biography [baɪ'ɒɡrəfɪ]   n. 传记；传记作品   U7b
◆blueprint ['bluːprɪnt]   n. 蓝图；行动方案；模型   U4a
blur [blɜː(r)]   v.（使）变得模糊不清；看不清
　　　　　　　n.（移动的）模糊形状；模糊的记忆   U7b
◆boom [buːm]   n. 激增；繁荣   U4a
brainwave ['breɪnweɪv]   n. 灵感；妙计；脑电波   U5a
brilliant ['brɪljənt]   a. 印象深刻的，闪光的，辉煌的   U2a
◆buoyant ['bɔɪənt]   a. 轻快的，活泼的；（指物体）能漂浮的；有浮力的   U7a
burden ['bɜːdn]   n.（义务、责任等的）重担；负担
　　　　　　　v.（使）担负（沉重或艰难的任务、职责等）   U1b
◆burgeoning ['bɜːdʒənɪŋ]   a. 迅猛发展的；急剧增长的   U4a

C

cancel ['kænsl]   v. 取消；撤销；终止；注销   U4a
◆captivate ['kæptɪveɪt]   v. 迷住；使着迷   U5b
carbon ['kɑːbən]   n. 碳   U3a
★career [kə'rɪə(r)]   n. 生涯；职业   U1b
cautious ['kɔːʃəs]   a. 小心的；谨慎的   U4b
★certificate [sə'tɪfɪkət]   n. 证明；证明书   U1a
chapter ['tʃæptə(r)]   n. 章；回；篇   U7b
◆claimant ['kleɪmənt]   n. 原告；（贸易）索赔人；提出要求者   U8b
◆cling [klɪŋ]   v. 抓紧，紧握，紧抱   U2a
◆comic ['kɒmɪk]   a. 使人发笑的；可笑的；滑稽的   U7b
★commit [kə'mɪt]   v. 做出（错或非法的事）；犯（罪或错等）   U4b
commonplace ['kɒmənpleɪs]   n. 寻常的事物，平常的东西   U2a

162

Appendix 2

communication [kə,mju:nɪˈkeɪʃn] n. 传递；传播；交流；交换；通信	U3a
★comparable [ˈkɒmpərəbl] a. 类似的；可比较的	U1b
★complaint [kəmˈpleɪnt] n. 抱怨；埋怨；投诉；控告	U4b
◆conceivable [kənˈsi:vəbl] a. 可想象的；可信的	U5a
conclusion [kənˈklu:ʒn] n. 结论；推论	U1b
condemned [kənˈdemd] a. 已被定罪的	U7a
◆confederate [kənˈfedərət] a. 联盟的；同盟的；邦联的	
n. 同伙；合谋者；同党	U6a
★confess [kənˈfes] v. 供认；坦白；承认；忏悔	U4b
confident [ˈkɒnfɪdənt] a. 自信的；有自信心的	U1a
★conflict [ˈkɒnflɪkt] n. 冲突；抵触	
v. 战斗；争执	U6a
★confront [kənˈfrʌnt] v. 面对；处理；解决	U2a
conscious [ˈkɒnʃəs] a. 感觉到的；意识到的；清醒的	U3a
★consultant [kənˈsʌltənt] n. 顾问；高级顾问医师；会诊医师	U4b
consume [kənˈsju:m] v. 消耗；耗费；吃；烧毁	U4b
contain [kənˈteɪn] v. 包含；容纳	U4b
◆criminal [ˈkrɪmɪnl] n. 罪犯，犯人	
a. 犯罪的，刑事上的	U7a
◆cripple [ˈkrɪpl] v. 使残废；严重毁坏（或损害）	
n. 残疾人；跛子	U4a
★critic [ˈkrɪtɪk] n. 批评家；评论家；评论员；挑剔的人	U4b
criticize [ˈkrɪtɪsaɪz] v. 批评；批判；评论；评价	U7b
★crystal [ˈkrɪstl] n. 水晶，石英晶体；晶体	U8a
a. 水晶制的，晶体的	
★cursor [ˈkɜ:sə(r)] n. （计算机荧光屏上的）光标；游标	U5a
◆customary [ˈkʌstəməri] a. 习惯的；习俗的；通常的	U6b

D

★decade [ˈdekeɪd] n. 十年；十年期（尤指一个年代）	U4a
definite [ˈdefɪnət] a. 明确的；确切的；肯定的	U7b
demonstrate [ˈdemənstreɪt] v. 证明；证实；表达；示范	U4b
designate [ˈdezɪgneɪt] v. 指明；指派；意味着；把……定名为	
a. 指定而尚未上任的；选出而尚未上任的	U8a

163

detect [dɪˈtekt]	v. 发现；查明；探测	U5a
◆detour [ˈdiːtʊə(r)]	n. 绕路，绕道	U2b
◆dictate [dɪkˈteɪt]	v. 口授；强行规定；摆布；指使	U7b
◆dismay [dɪsˈmeɪ]	n. 沮丧；绝望	
	v. 使……沮丧；使…绝望	U2b
★dispose [dɪˈspəʊz]	v. (of) 丢掉，消除	U3b
★distinct [dɪˈstɪŋkt]	a. 截然不同的；清楚的；明显的	U7b
division [dɪˈvɪʒn]	n. 分裂；分开；分配；除（法）	U6a
divorce [dɪˈvɔːs]	n. 离婚	U1a
	a. 与（某人）离婚；判（某人）离婚	
domestic [dəˈmestɪk]	n. 家庭纠纷；家庭矛盾	
	a. 本国的；国内的；家庭的；驯养的	U4a
◆doom [dum; duːm]	n. 死亡；毁灭；劫数	
	v. 注定某人（死亡、毁灭、失败等）	U7a

E

◆ecological [ˌiːkəˈlɒdʒɪkl]	a. 生态的；生态学的	U3b
economy [ɪˈkɒnəmɪ]	n. 经济；经济情况；经济结构	U1b
element [ˈelɪmənt]	n. 成分；要素；元素	U7b
◆emancipation [ɪˌmænsɪˈpeɪʃn]	n. （从束缚、支配下）解放	U6a
◆embed [ɪmˈbed]	v. 把……牢牢地嵌入（或插入、埋入）	U5a
emerge [ɪˈmɜːdʒ]	v. 出现，浮现，露出	U2b
enthusiast [ɪnˈθjuːzɪæst]	n. 爱好者；热衷者；热心人	U6b
★environmental [ɪnˌvaɪərənˈmentl]	a. 个人环境的；由个人环境产生的；环境的	U3a
★environmentally [ɪnˌvaɪərənˈmentəlɪ]	ad. 有关环境方面；环境地	U3a
◆epilepsy [ˈepɪlepsɪ]	n. 癫痫	U5a
★equivalent [ɪˈkwɪvələnt]	a. 相当的；相等的；等值的 n. 相等物	U6a
◆erratic [ɪˈrætɪk]	a. 不规则的；不确定的；不稳定的；不可靠的	U4a
★eventual [ɪˈventʃuːəl]	a. 最终的，最后的	U2a
everlasting [ˌevəˈlɑːstɪŋ]	a. 永久的；永恒的	U1a
★evolutionary [ˌiːvəˈluːʃənrɪ]	a. 进化的；演变的	U5b
★excess [ɪkˈses]	n. 超过；过度；过分；放肆行为	U4a
	a. 超额的；额外的；附加的	
exhibition [ˌeksɪˈbɪʃn]	n. 陈列，展览； 展览品	U8a

Appendix 2

★expansion [ɪk'spænʃn] *n.* 扩张；扩展；扩大；膨胀   U4a
　expansion [ɪk'spænʃn] *n.* 扩张；膨胀；扩大   U6b
　expense [ɪk'spens] *n.* 费用；价钱   U1b
　expert ['ekspɜːt] *a.* 熟练的；内行的
　　　　　　　　　　n. 专家；能手   U6a

F

★faculty ['fæklti] *n.* 才能，能力；大学的系，科，院；全体从业人员 U7a
◆fairytale ['feərɪteɪl] *a.* 童话式的，童话中才有的，优美无比的   U8a
　favourable ['feɪvərəbl] *a.* 给人好印象的；赞同的   U1b
★feasible ['fiːzəbl] *a.* 可行的；行得通的   U1b
　fiction ['fɪkʃn] *n.* 小说；虚构的事   U7b
★financial [faɪ'nænʃl] *a.* 财政的；财务的   U1b
★financial [faɪnænʃl] *a.* 金融的   U2b
　flash [flæʃ] *n.* 闪光；闪耀
　　　　　　　v. （使）闪耀，闪光；用光发出信号   U1a
◆flatter ['flætə(r)] *v.* 恭维；奉承；讨好（某人）   U7b
◆flaw [flɔː] *n.* 错误；缺点；裂痕；瑕疵   U4b

G

　gamble ['gæmbl] *v.* （牌戏、赛马等中）赌博，打赌
　　　　　　　　　n. 赌博；打赌；冒险   U1a
◆gear [gɪə(r)] *n.* 排挡；齿轮
　　　　　　　v. 使与……相适应   U5b
◆gesticulate [dʒe'stɪkjuleɪt] *v.* 做手势；用手势表达；用动作示意 U5a
　glance [glɑːns] *n.* 匆匆一看，一瞥，扫视   U2a
★global ['gləʊbl] *a.* 全球性的；全世界的；包括一切的   U3a
◆grandeur ['grændʒə(r)] *n.* 宏伟，壮丽，堂皇   U2a
★grant [grɑːnt] *n.* 拨款
　　　　　　　v. 授予；同意；准予   U6a
　grocery ['grəʊsəri] *n.* 食品杂货店；食品杂货业   U3a
　grown-up [grəʊn ʌp] *n.* 大人；成人
　　　　　　　　　　　a. 成熟的；成年的；长大的   U4b
　guarantee [ˌgærən'tiː] *n.* 保证；担保

165

	v. 保证；担保	U1a
◆gurney [gɜːnɪ]	n.（医院中推送病人用的）轮床	U2a

H

◆habitual [həbɪtʃuəl]	a. 习惯的；惯常的；习以为常的	U8b
◆heal [hiːl]	v. 愈合；治愈；（使）结束；消除	U6a
healthy ['helθɪ]	a. 健康的；强健的	U3a
◆hectic ['hektɪk]	a. 忙碌的，繁忙的	U1a
heritage ['herɪtɪdʒ]	n. 遗产；继承物；传统	U6b
hesitate ['hezɪteɪt]	v. 犹豫；（对某事）迟疑不决	U1b
★hint [hɪnt]	n. 暗示；示意；(pl.) 建议；提示	U7b
historian [hɪˈstɔːrɪən]	n. 历史学家；史学工作者	U6a
★hospitalize ['hɒspɪtəlaɪz]	v. 送（某人）入院治疗	U2a

I

◆impact ['ɪmpækt]	v.（对某事物）有影响；有作用；冲击；撞击	
	n. 巨大影响；强大作用；撞击；冲击力	U4a
◆impairment [ɪmˈpeəmənt]	n. 故障；缺陷；损害，损伤	U7a
◆impalpable [ɪmˈpælpəbl]	a. 感触不到的；摸不到的；难解的	U7b
◆impending [ɪmˈpendɪŋ]	a. 即将发生的；迫在眉睫的	U7a
◆imperceptible [ˌɪmpəˈseptəbl]	a. 无法察觉的；感觉不到的	U7b
◆implant ['ɪmplɑːnt]	n.（植入人体中的）植入物	U5a
[ɪmˈplɑːnt]	v. 灌输；将……植入	
indifferent [ɪnˈdɪfrənt]	a. 漠不关心的，不感兴趣的	U2a
★inevitability [ɪnˌevɪtəˈbɪlətɪ]	n. 必然性	U2a
★insight ['ɪnsaɪt]	n. 洞察力；领悟	U2a
instruct [ɪnˈstrʌkt]	v. 指示，命令，吩咐	U2a
◆intake ['ɪnteɪk]	n. 吸入，纳入（液体、气体等）	U3a
◆integrity [ɪnˈtegrətɪ]	n. 正直，诚实；完整	U8b
intelligent [ɪnˈtelɪdʒənt]	a. 聪明的；理解力强的；有智力的	U8b
intend [ɪnˈtend]	v. 打算；计划；想要	U1a
intensive [ɪnˈtensɪv]	a. 密集的；彻底的；十分细致的	U2a
◆interactive [ˌɪntərˈæktɪv]	a. 合作的；相互影响的；互动的	U5b
◆interface ['ɪntəfeɪs]	n.（人机）界面；接口	U5a

166

Appendix 2

          v. 接合；连接
★interpretation [ɪn,tɜːprɪˈteɪʃn] *n.* 翻译；口译；解释；说明 U6a

K

◆keenness [kiːnes] *n.* 敏锐 U7a
◆keypad [ˈkiːpæd] *n.* 小键盘；按键 U5a

L

◆legacy [ˈleɡəsɪ] *n.* 遗产，遗赠；遗留问题；后遗 U2b
◆lethargy [ˈleθədʒɪ] *n.* 昏睡；倦怠；无精打采 U7a
 lifestyle [ˈlaɪfstaɪl] *n.* 生活方式 U3a

M

◆manifold [ˈmænɪfəʊld] *a.* 繁多的，多种的；多方面的；多种形式的 U7a
◆manuscript [ˈmænjuskrɪpt] *n.* 手稿；原稿；底稿 U8a
 marathon [ˈmærəθən] *n.* 马拉松赛跑（距离约42公里，合26英里） U1a
 marriage [ˈmærɪdʒ] *n.* 结婚；婚姻 U1a
◆martial [ˈmɑːʃl] *a.* 武术的；军事的 U6b
★marvelous [ˈmɑːvələs] *a.* 极好的，非凡的 U2a
 massive [ˈmæsɪv] *a.* 巨大的；大而重的；结实的 U3b
 mellow [ˈmeləʊ] *a.* 熟透的；芳醇的；(人格、思想等)老练的，成熟的； U7a
◆methane [ˈmiːθeɪn] *n.* 甲烷；沼气 U3a
 migrant [ˈmaɪɡrənt] *n.* 移居者；移民 U8b
 military [ˈmɪlətrɪ] *a.* 军事的，军用的 U6a
◆mortal [ˈmɔːtl] *a.* 终有一死的；有深仇大恨的；不共戴天的 U7a
◆mortgage [ˈmɔːɡɪdʒ] *v.* 按揭（由银行等提供房产抵押借款） U1b
★motion [ˈməʊʃn] *n.* 运动；动作 U5b
◆moviegoer [ˈmuːvɪɡəʊə(r)] *n.* （经常）上电影院的人；爱看电影者 U5b
◆mumbo-jumbo [,mʌmbəʊ-ˈdʒʌmbəʊ] *n.* 胡言乱语；繁文缛节 U5a
◆mutuality [,mjuːtʃuˈælətɪ] *n.* 相互关系；相关 U6a

N

★narrative [ˈnærətɪv] *n.* 故事；记叙文；叙述；讲述 U6a
 necessitate [nəˈsesɪteɪt] *v.* 使……成为必要，需要 U6a

negative ['negətɪv] *a.* 负面的；坏的；否定的		U3b
★neutral ['nju:trəl] *a.* 中立的；不偏不倚的；神经的；神经系统的		U3a

O

◆obstacle ['ɒbstəkl] *n.* 障碍；阻碍		U1a
official [ə'fɪʃl] *n.* 要员；官员；高级职员		
a. 公务的；公职的；正式的；官方的		U4a
◆offset ['ɒfset] *v.* 补偿或抵消某事物		U3a
n. 胶印法		
◆omnivore ['ɒmnɪvɔ:(r)] *n.* 杂食动物；杂食者		U3a
option ['ɒpʃn] *n.* 可选择的事物；选择；选择权		U1b
◆ordain [ɔ:'deɪn] *v.* 主宰，掌握，注定		U2a
★original [ə'rɪdʒənl] *a.* 原始的；最初的；独创的；新颖的		U6b
◆outfit ['aʊtfɪt] *n.* 全套服装；团队		
v. 装备；配置设备		U5a

P

◆panorama [ˌpænə'rɑ:mə] *n.* 风景的全貌		U7a
◆paradox ['pærədɒks] *n.* 矛盾的人（或事物、情况）		U2a
partner ['pɑ:tnə(r)] *n.* 配偶；同伴		U1a
payment ['peɪmənt] *n.* 付款；支付		U1b
pension ['penʃn] *n.* 退休金，养老金		U8b
★permanent ['pɜ:mənənt] *a.* 永久性的，耐久的，固定不变的		U7a
◆petty ['peti] *a.* 小的，琐碎的，不重要的		U2a
★phase [feɪz] *n.* 阶段；时期		
v. 分阶段进行；逐步做		U5b
★philosophy [fə'lɒsəfi] *n.* 哲学；人生哲学；主旨		U6b
◆pinpoint ['pɪnpɔɪnt] *v.* 确定，准确地指出；精准定位		U2b
poetry ['pəʊətri] *n.* 诗歌；诗集		U7b
poisonous ['pɔɪzənəs] *a.* 引起中毒的；有毒的		U3b
popularity [ˌpɒpju'lærəti] *n.* 受欢迎；普及；流行		U5b
◆pore [pɔ:(r)] *n.* 毛孔，气孔，细孔		U2a
pose [pəʊz] *v.* 引起；产生；造成（威胁，问题等）		
n. （为画像，拍照等摆的）姿势		U3b

Appendix 2

potential [pə'tenʃl] *n.* 可能性；潜在性；潜力；潜质		
a. 潜在的；可能的		U4a
pour[pɔ:(r)] *v.* 使（液体）连续流出；倾倒；倒出		U3b
precious ['preʃəs] *a.* 珍奇的，宝贵的，珍贵的		U2a
◆preconception [,pri:kən'sepʃn] *n.* 预想；成见；事先形成的观念		U7b
prejudice ['predʒudɪs] *n.* 偏见；成见		U7b
★preoccupy [prɪ'ɒkjupaɪ] *v.* 使日夜思考，使忧心忡忡		U2a
★priority[praɪ'ɒrəti] *n.* 优先，在前		U2b
promising ['prɒmɪsɪŋ] *a.* 有希望的；有前途的；有出息的		U5b
◆prowess ['praʊəs] *n.* 非凡的技能；高超的技艺；造诣		U4b

Q

quantity ['kwɒntəti]   *n.* 量；大小；重量；数目；数量   U3a

R

range [reɪndʒ] *n.* 范围；幅度；距离；一系列		
v. 延伸；（在某范围内）变化		U6b
recognize ['rekəgnaɪz] *v.* 认识，认出，辨别出		U2a
recycle [,ri:'saɪkl] *v.* 回收利用；再利用		U3b
◆reduction [rɪ'dʌkʃn] *n.* 缩减；降低；简化；还原		U3a
reflect [rɪ'flekt] *v.* 体现；反映；反射；反省		U6b
region ['ri:dʒən] *n.* 地区；区域；行政区		U5a
release [rɪ'li:s] *n.* 释放；发布；发行		U5a
◆relive [,ri:'lɪv] *v.* （尤指在想象中）再次体验，重温；回味		U1a
◆resonate ['rezəneɪt] *v.* 产生回声、共鸣或共振		U6a
resort [rɪ'zɔ:t] *v.* 求助于或诉诸某事物		
n. 求助；娱乐场，度假胜地；采用的办法		U8a
risk [rɪsk] *n.* 危险；风险		
v. 使……冒风险（或面临危险）		U1a
◆robust [rəʊ'bʌst] *a.* 精力充沛的；坚定的；粗野的		U8b
roll [rəʊl] *v.* 滚动，滚落，翻落；使摇摆，使摇晃；碾；绕，卷		
n. 一卷，卷状物；面包卷；名单，名册		U2b
roughly ['rʌfli] *ad.* 大约；大致		U1b
route [ru:t] *n.*（公共汽车和列车等的）常规路线；固定线路；路途；渠道		U4a

S

★sacrifice['sækrɪfaɪs]　　v. 牺牲，把……奉献给……；廉价卖出；牺牲，献祭　　U2b
　scare [skeə(r)]　　v. 惊吓；使害怕；使恐惧
　　　　　　　　　　n. 恐慌；恐惧；惊吓；惊恐　　U4b
★scattered ['skætəd]　　a. 分散的；零散的；疏落的　　U5a
◆scatty ['skætɪ]　　a. 健忘的；傻乎乎的　　U4b
★scheme [skiːm]　　n. 计划；方案；阴谋；诡计　　U3a
★secede [sɪ'siːd]　　v. 脱离；退出　　U6a
★severe [sɪ'vɪə(r)]　　a. 极为恶劣的，十分严重的　　U2a
★significant [sɪg'nɪfɪkənt]　　a. 有重大意义的；显著的；意味深长的　　U4a
★slavery ['sleɪvərɪ]　　n. 蓄奴制；奴隶制度；奴隶身份　　U6a
◆sleek [sliːk]　　v. 使（头发等）发油光；使平整光亮
　　　　　　　　　a. 光滑的；光亮的；线条流畅的；造型优美的　　U4a
◆slur [slɜː(r)]　　v. 诽谤；诋毁；污辱；含糊不清地说话　　U4b
　　　　　　　　n. 诽谤；诋毁；污辱
◆sparkling [spɑːklɪŋ]　　a. 闪烁的，闪耀的　　U2a
★specify ['spesɪfaɪ]　　v. 指定；详细说明　　U7a
★sphere [sfɪə(r)]　　n.（某人的活动、兴趣、影响等的）范围；球，球体　　U7a
◆spooky ['spuːkɪ]　　a. 怪异吓人的　　U5a
◆spouse [spaʊs]　　n. 配偶；夫或妻　　U2a
◆stability [stə'bɪlətɪ]　　n. 稳定（性）；稳固（性）　　U1b
　stable['steɪbl]　　a. 稳定的；稳固的　　U1b
　steak [steɪk]　　n. 肉排；鱼排；（尤指）牛排　　U3a
　steep [stiːp]　　a. 陡峭的；陡直的
　　　　　　　　v. 深深浸泡；饱含（某品质）　　U7b
★stimulation [,stɪmju'leɪʃn]　　n. 刺激　　U5b
◆stray [streɪ]　　v. 走失；偏离正题；（已婚者或有固定关系者）有外遇　　U2b
★stretch [stretʃ]　　n. 一段时间，一段路程；伸展，扩张
　　　　　　　　　　v. 拉伸；伸展　　U7a
◆strive [straɪv]　　v. 努力奋斗，力求；斗争，力争　　U2b
◆subconscious [,sʌb'kɒnʃəs]　　a. 下意识的；潜意识的　　U4b
　suitable ['suːtəbl]　　a. 合适的；适宜的　　U1a
◆suppress [sə'pres]　　v. 禁止发表；抑制；压制；镇压　　U6a

★surgical [ˈsɜːdʒɪkl]   *a.* 外科的；外科手术的   U5a
　surrender [səˈrendə(r)]   *v.* 投降；放弃
　　　　　　　　　　n. 放弃；屈服；投降   U6a
◆sustainable [səˈsteɪnəbl]   *a.* 可持续的；可忍受的；可支撑的   U3a
◆synchronized [ˈsɪŋkrənaɪzd]   *a.* 同步的   U8a

T

★technique [tekˈniːk]   *n.* 技巧；工艺；技术   U5b
★technology [tekˈnɒlədʒɪ]   *n.* 科技（总称）；工业技术；工艺学   U8a
◆telepathy [təˈlepəθɪ]   *n.* 传心术；通灵术；心灵感应   U5a
★tend [tend]   *v.* 往往会；常常就；趋向   U1a
◆therapeutic [ˌθerəˈpjuːtɪk]   *a.* 治疗的；医疗的；有助于放松精神的   U5a
★threat [θret]   *n.* 威胁；恐吓；凶兆；形成威胁的事物   U4a
◆thrill [θrɪl]   *n.* 兴奋感；激动
　　　　　　 v. 使非常兴奋；使非常激动   U5b
◆thrilling [ˈθrɪlɪŋ]   *a.* 惊心动魄的；使人激动的；毛骨悚然的   U7a
◆toll [təʊl]   *v.* 敲（钟）；（尤指）鸣（丧钟）
　　　　　 n. （道路、桥梁等的）通行费；毁坏；伤亡人数   U4a
★tone [təʊn]   *n.* 腔调；语气；风气；气氛   U7b
★track [træk]   *v.* 跟随；留下痕迹
　　　　　　 n. 崎岖不平的小路；火车；轨道；方向   U4a
◆tragic [ˈtrædʒɪk]   *a.* 可悲的；悲痛的   U7b
　transform [trænsˈfɔːm]   *v.* 改变；改造；改革   U6a
　transport [ˈtrænspɔːt]   *v.* 运送，运输
　　　　　　　　　 n. 运输   U8a
★troop [truːp]   *n.* 军队；部队；一群；一队   U6a
　twist [twɪst]   *v.* 使扭曲；扭曲变形
　　　　　　 n. 转动；扭动   U7b

U

★ultimately [ˈʌltɪmətlɪ]   *ad.* 最终，最后，终归   U2a
　uncertainty [ʌnˈsɜːtntɪ]   *n.* 犹豫；迟疑   U1b
　undergo [ˌʌndəˈgəʊ]   *v.* 经历；经受   U5b
★uniform [ˈjuːnɪfɔːm]   *n.* 制服；军服   U4a

unlimited [ʌn'lɪmɪtɪd]　*a.* 尽量多的；任意多的；无限制的　　U3b

V

◆ vegetarian [ˌvedʒɪ'teərɪən]　*n.* 吃素的人　　U3a
◆ vendor ['vendə(r)]　*n.* 小贩；摊贩；卖方；供应商　　U4a
　 vigor ['vɪgə(r)]　*n.* 体力；精力；活力　　U7a
◆ vow [vaʊ]　*v.* 起誓；发誓；郑重宣告　　U6a
　　　　　　n. 誓言；郑重宣布；许愿

W

◆ wedlock ['wedlɒk]　*n.* 婚姻；已婚状态　　U1a
◆ womb [wuːm]　*n.* 子宫　　U2a

Y

　 youngster ['jʌŋstə(r)]　*n.* 年轻人；少年；儿童　　U4b

Phrases and Expressions

a series of　一系列；一连串　　U8a
according to　根据，依据　　U8a
add up to　总计达；意味着　　U1b
afford to do　支付得起；（买）得起（某物）　　U1b
all but　几乎，差不多　　U7a
all too often　时常　　U2a
apply to　适用于；运用；致力于；　　U8a
as much as　差不多　　U3a
aside from　除……之外；既……又……　　U6b
at ease　舒适；自在；无拘无束　　U4b
at the end of　在……结尾；在……末端　　U3a
be guaranteed to do sth.　必定做某事　　U1a
be located in　坐落于，位于　　U2a
be satisfied with　对……感到满意　　U1b
behind the wheel　在驾驶；在操舵；控制；掌管　　U4b
break through　突围；突破　　U2a

Appendix 2

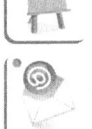

carry out 执行；实现；完成	U4b
◆cling to 保留；紧抓；坚持	U2a
come a long way 取得进展；明显提高	U6a
comment on 评论；注释	U4b
compare to 把……比作	U8b
compare with 与……相比较	U1a
contribute to 促成；有助于	U8b
crowd into 大批涌入（某狭小空间）	U7a
cut down 砍倒，删减，击倒，杀死	U3b
emerge from (sth.) （从困境或苦难经历中）幸存下来；摆脱出来	U4a
fall in love 相爱	U1a
figure out 计算出，弄明白，解决，合计	U2b
focus on 致力于；集中于	U6a
freak out 疯狂、兴奋的感受（尤指因毒品所致）	U2b
get married 结婚	U1a
◆gear sth. towards/to sth. 使与……相适应；使适合于	U5b
give off 发出（光等），放出，散发	U3b
give up 放弃；放手	U2a
guarantee sth (to sb) 向某人保证某事	U1a
have a taste of 体会；领略	U8a
have impact on 对……有影响	U3a
have the time for…to do sth. 有时间做某事	U1a
◆hang back 退缩不前	U7b
hesitate to do sth. 做某事迟疑	U1b
in conclusion 最后，总之	U1b
in contrast 相比之下	U4a
in effect 实际上，事实上	U3a
in one's point 在某人看来	U1a
in particular 特别；尤其	U6b
in place 在适当的位置；适当的；在工作	U8b
in short 简而言之；总之	U3a
in some cases 在一些情况下	U1b
in the case of 至于；就……而言；在……情况下	U4a
intend to do sth. 打算做某事	U1a

173

interest rate 利率；利息	U1b
involve in 参与；涉及；使进入；使卷入	U3a
let go 放开；释放；发射	U2a
look on sth./sb. with sth. (以某种方式) 看待	U4a
makes it clear 弄清楚；讲明	U4a
marathon dating 马拉松式约会	U1a
motion picture 电影	U5b
no matter whether 无论是否……(都不要紧)	U1a
no more 不再	U2a
pour into 川流不息地涌入，源源而来	U3b
prevent from 防止	U7b
pull into (车、船等) 驶入	U4a
push back 推出；使撤退，使回到原处	U2b
put into 输入，使进入，把……译成，表达	U3b
refer to…as… 把……称为；认为……是	U6b
science-fiction novel 科幻小说	U5a
separate from 与……分离	U7b
settle down 定居，过安定生活	U1b
spend…(in) doing sth. 花……（时间、金钱等）做某事	U1a
state-of-the-art 最先进的	U5b
stretch out （使某事物）延续或足够所需	U7a
take advantage of 利用	U8b
take into account 考虑到；顾及	U4a
take sb./sth. for granted 因熟悉某（某事物）而觉察不出真正价值；认为理当如此	U7a
◆tap into 利用，开发，发掘	U5b
tear apart 使……分裂；把……痛苦地分开；把……弄乱	U6a
tend to 往往会；倾向于；易于	U6b
to and fro 来回地；往复地	U2a
to…extent 到……程度；在……程度上	U5a
translate into （把……）翻译成……；把……转化成	U6b
turn into （使）变成；译成；成为	U8a
voice it all out 大声说出来	U2b
well over 多余；超过	U6a